TUBULAR
Therapy

Debbie Sempsrott & Denise Rogers

WESTBOW°
PRESS
A DIVISION OF THOMAS NELSON
& ZONDERVAN

"Scripture quotations labeled (NIV) are from the Holy Bible, New International Version®, NIV® Copyright © 1973, 1978, 1984, 2011 by Biblica, Inc.® Used by permission. All rights reserved worldwide."

"Scripture quotations marked (NLT) are taken from the Holy Bible, New Living Translation, copyright © 1996, 2004, 2007 by Tyndale House Foundation. Used by permission of Tyndale House Publishers, Inc., Carol Stream, Illinois 60188. All rights reserved."

"Scripture taken from *The Message*. Copyright © 1993, 1994, 1995, 1996, 2000, 2001, 2002. Used by permission of NavPress Publishing Group."
Edited by Vicki White

Graphics used with permission by Gretchen Jackson.

WestBow Press books may be ordered through booksellers or by contacting:
WestBow Press
A Division of Thomas Nelson & Zondervan
1663 Liberty Drive
Bloomington, IN 47403
www.westbowpress.com
1 (866) 928-1240

ISBN: 978-1-4908-3911-0 (sc)
ISBN: 978-1-4908-3912-7 (hc)
ISBN: 978-1-4908-3910-3 (e)
Library of Congress Control Number: 2014909987

Printed in the United States of America.

WestBow Press rev. date: 6/12/2014

Readers Beware!

What readers are saying about Debbie & Denise's first book,
Happy Dance:

- **Lydia feels lighter**—*"This book will lower your blood pressure while waiting in a dentist or doctor's office...so I keep a copy in my purse!"*
- **Husbands, TOO!**—*"My husband picked up this book first and said, 'You've got to stop and listen to this?' He read me the entire first chapter. What a delightful, tender book for women and their listening husbands."*
- **MJ's Hooray**—*"This is a great book...encouraging and funny. The combination of both ladies is what makes it. I can't wait for another."*
- **Be Warned!**—*"I laughed until the tears ran down my legs! People stared at me due to the snorting and loss of breath. What a fun, inspiring book."*
- **Laughing Out Loud in CA**—*"This was an inspiring book that had me laughing from start to finish. Easy read. I couldn't put it down and can't wait to read the next books! Beware of reading this in public places!"*
- **Kicking Cancer**—*"It will make you laugh. It will make you cry. It will make you laugh until you cry. These words of truth from women to women will feed your soul and calm your spirit."*
- **Jail Break**—*"The women in prison can't wait until we bring more books. They are laughing, listening, and learning."*

So, Readers Beware! This book may lower your blood pressure, make you laugh in public places, and lighten your load of cares... Good news girls!! We're back with more LOL stories! It's totally tubular fun as we look at the story of faith and friendship triumphing over fear.

We call it Tubular Therapy.

Contents

Acknowledgements

"The best things in life come in threes, like friends, dreams, and memories."
--Author Unknown

We would like to dedicate this book to all the people who have "kept us afloat" through the many different seasons of our lives. These people are not always up-front, noticed, or thanked enough. They are the ones that point us to God and show us His love through their touch given on His behalf. They bless us with their smiles, their presence, and a "hand up" that helps us run the race toward our eternal goal. We call them family, mentors, friends, and BFFs. The gift of love they give is one that will last for all eternity.

We especially give thanks for our families. Their smiles, hugs, and daily support are the highlights of our lives. Our first and last words of each and every day are prayers of thanksgiving for our greatest gifts in life, our families!

Denise and I give special thanks for our editor and friend, Vicki White. She not only brings us the gift of editing, but she is the third cord in our "strand of gold". Not only is she an awesome friend but she is a mighty prayer warrior.

We have laughed and smiled at all of the sketches created of us and for us by Gretchen Jackson. Thank you, Gretchen, for sharing your gift with us.

This book is dedicated to all of our very special, amazing, "totally tubular" friends!

> "Though one may be overpowered, two can defend themselves. A cord of three strands is not quickly broken." (Ecclesiastes 4:12 NIV)

Preface

Funny Denise

Ever have one of those moments you can't get out of your head no matter how hard you try? Just the thought of it can cause you to giggle even if you are in an important meeting with doctors or lawyers discussing bookkeeping practices or unpaid taxes. You know it isn't the appropriate time to laugh, but you really can't help it. The image in your mind just takes you away to the long forgotten fun side of your brain.

One such moment is stored on my phone for easy viewing on those days when I have simply forgotten how to laugh. This little video was made during a getaway to a lazy river with my co-author and best friend, Debbie.

We were talking and relaxing by the pool with her daughter, simply watching the empty tubes float by. Debbie seemed to grow momentarily quiet as a cluster of tubes came around the bend just above where we were sitting. Suddenly, Debbie said, "Do you think I can jump from here and make it into that tube?"

Now, I am from Texas, so I am accustomed to hearing people saying things like, "Hey, y'all ... watch this!" I didn't know what to expect, but I knew it was going to be good. I am one of the few people on this planet who knows Debbie is one *cuh-RAY-zee* girl, so not wanting to miss a good show, I said, "Nope, I don't think you can, but if you do I'll give you twenty bucks." This was a long shot and I was feeling pretty safe. I am a reasonable, logical kind of person. Debbie, however, is not. (That is one of the things I love most about her.)

In the next instant, Debbie had blasted off from her chair and propelled herself clear across the lazy river, executing a perfect, tushy-first landing in the nearest floating yellow tube. She floated away hooting with laughter and holding up her arms in a victory salute.

If tube jumping and tushy-landing were an Olympic sport, Debbie would be a contender! We were busting a gut, howling with laughter, and I laugh again every time I think about it.

How many sober, fifty-something women have you seen leaping through the air lately? Exactly! And of that small population sample, how many of those are pastors' wives? Debbie is definitely one of a kind.

Realist that I am, I asked her if she could do it again so I could capture it on video. I am no fool. I knew how much money I could make on one of those shows where you send in a funny home video. This was my golden ticket!

Never one to shrink from a dare, she said, "Sure, I can do it again."

Everyone has her pegged as the demure little pastor's wife sitting in her church pew, but she is really more comfortable pretending she's a member of Cirque du Soleil, flying through the air and aiming for an inner tube. As promised, she did it perfectly a second time with complete abandon and joy, landing her tushy right in the middle of that yellow tube. She was ecstatic! Debbie just loves to push the envelope, or the proverbial tube, as the case may be. All you can hear on the video is me laughing loud and hard. Just thinking about it now makes me chuckle.

I, on the other hand, am the one who can't get my tushy *out* of the tube once it has become stuck in there … but we will save that story for another time.

The truth is simply this: we all get stuck sometimes, and we may just need a little push to get us going again. Other times, we just need to let go of our fears and take a leap of faith. Regardless of where we are in life, there are some times when we are all in need of a float, friendship, and the freedom that comes with laughter.

Tubular Therapy is the new rage in counseling. Yes ladies, you, too, can trade in the couch for the floating tube. Before you think we are lunatics (you ladies are pretty sharp!) we just want you to consider the possibility that there truly is healing in friendship, relaxation, and laughter. Christian counseling is awesome, but most of us not only need wise counsel, we need a friend who will walk through life with us. We are two crazy best friends who want to share a few ways we have grown in our walk with God, our relationships, and our sanity, while floating ... simply floating through the seasons of life together.

When God reaches down to earth to shower us with His unmerited favor and grace, He often uses human hands. He sent His son to give us His amazing grace, and He entrusted ordinary people to heal the sick and lift up the fallen. God is still in the same business today. His love simply encircles us like a big ol' inner tube. It surrounds us, insulates us, protects us and keeps us afloat. The Bible calls it "unconditional love"; we call it *Tubular Therapy.*

No matter what season you find yourself in, you will be uplifted as we float together. We are going to chat about those funny things that most people would never dare say out loud, especially pastors' wives. Yet those thoughts are always in the back of our minds. Perhaps if we are honest and real with all of you, then you too will have the courage to share with someone else your struggles. It's ok to struggle; after the struggle we will experience new strength. We hope you find hilarity, hope, and healing as we float together.

> "A cheerful disposition is good medicine for your health; Gloom and doom leave you bone tired."
> (Proverbs 17: 22 The Message)

CHAPTER ONE

Two Crazy Friends

Denise Rogers & Debbie Sempsrott:
"Our Faith Floats"

*"Friends love through all kinds of weather, and families
stick together in all kinds of trouble."
(Proverbs 17:17 The Message)*

Tubular Therapy

Meet "Just Debbie"
Denise Rogers

Debbie is a preacher's wife and a preacher's kid. I guess I could stop right there, and you would think you knew all about her. You would think she is perfect in everything she thinks, says, and does and that she only cracks a smile to be polite to others. Well, you would be wrong—you would be utterly and absolutely wrong. Let me introduce you to the real Debbie.

Visualize the girl you knew when you were growing up who always smelled of Coppertone, lived in a swimsuit from the first day of summer until school started in the fall, and was an expert with a rope over a lake and a tube in a pool. She usually had a mischievous look on her face, was smart as a whip (though she didn't want anyone to know it), and her ideal day was having fun in the sun. That's Debbie both then and now.

She also has the ability to pull together any event with the most beautiful décor. She can plan any trip or vacation, filling each day with fun, fabulous food, and the best swimming pool or lazy river you can imagine. She leads the music ministry with style and grace, puts together a children's ministry to be envied by all, and has developed a successful women's ministry from pretty much nothing.

Debbie is not only the preacher's wife; she is "Just Debbie." What I mean is that most preachers' wives are often known through their husbands, but Debbie has her own style. Let me share a few stories to clarify.

The first time I heard Debbie speak she talked about a trip she took with her youth group as a teenager where they visited different churches. Sometimes they didn't stay in people's homes, so getting a shower was often a challenge. Now, Debbie really likes to be clean, so she politely (and quietly) put on her swimsuit, took her shampoo and conditioner to the baptistery, and took a bath—bubbles and all! When caught, her answer was, "This *is* my Father's house, right? He would want me to be clean, wouldn't He?"

Another interesting thing about Debbie is that she is directionally challenged in more ways than I can possibly convey within the pages of a book. The first time we went on a Women of Faith trip to Anaheim we parked in a parking garage. I learned a valuable lesson about Debbie that day: don't *ever* let her park her car alone. She will never, and I mean *never*, remember where she parked. I guess you could say Debbie is a great spiritual leader in more ways than one because she's led us through so many prayers as we walked endless miles in all possible directions looking for her vehicle.

On this excursion to Anaheim she also had a ticket to exit the parking garage. The van was full of women leaving dinner and heading to the big event. I was in the seat directly behind hers, and as we pulled up to the machine, all she had to do was insert the card into the reader. Sounds easy, right? Not so easy for Debbie.

The card reader had a vertical slot for the exit card. I honestly didn't know you could insert a card so many wrong ways. There, of course, was a picture of how to properly insert the card, but visual directions didn't even help. She inserted the card facing to the right, facing to the left as we yelled orders on how to insert it and turn it around. She even turned it sideways and tried to put it in horizontally in a vertical card reader! This was our first glimpse of the *real* Debbie.

Debbie now has a GPS. That's certainly an important item in her life, but she also needs a copilot to read and interpret the map. I happen to be the lucky soul who is usually her copilot. I hate to drive and she hates to deal with the GPS, so we're a good fit. Well, I'd say it's a good fit ... except on this one particular trip.

The van was once again full of women all talking away when Debbie found herself lost in downtown San Diego. Now, for those of you who don't know San Diego, it's full of one way streets. We were looking for the Coronado Bridge. The GPS was directing us, and as any good copilot would be, I was totally focused on the directions we needed to follow to get to the bridge. According to the GPS, we needed to take a right on the next street.

As we approached the intersection as shown on the GPS map, I said to Debbie, "Hang a right." As she turned, I looked up and saw a sign that said, "No Driving on Railroad Tracks."

I thought, *How weird to have a sign like that in downtown San Diego.* As we turned the corner, the once laughing and cackling women fell silent. Debbie gripped the shuddering steering wheel as though her life depended on it as the entire van began rapidly bouncing up and down as if we were in an earthquake.

In a calm, deliberate, but shaky voice, Debbie looked at me and said, "Umm, there are *no* cars on this road."

Bouncing up and down in my seat with my eyes fixed on the GPS, I reiterated, "The GPS said we can go this way."

From the back seat we heard, "Railroad tracks! Turn right!"

Now you know why Debbie's van is full for every trip. Ladies line up for each and every adventure! Many a well-meaning soul has pointed out that Debbie and I are a lot like Lucy and Ethel. While it is true that I have the red hair and the antics of Lucy, it is Debbie who will take us on many unforgettable adventures. She makes me laugh, and as you read our stories, I think you will too. As she would tell you, she is "Just Debbie."

Tubular Therapy

Meet "Funny Denise"
Debbie Sempsrott

Picture yourself glued to your television screen. The music comes on as the big heart opens up, emblazoned with the words "I Love Lucy!" People still laugh until they cry watching Lucy grab chocolates off the conveyer belt and hide them in her hat. We still love to watch it just to see what crazy trouble Lucy gets into each episode even years after the show ended. Whether stomping grapes or starring in a commercial for "Vitameatavegamin," she stole our hearts. What would Lucy do without Ethel to help her get into all that trouble? What would Ethel do without Lucy?

For all practical purposes, I am pretty much Ethel to "Funny Denise," the crazy redhead whom we all love. That's what we call her at my house, anyway. She never meets a stranger. She will be the first one at church to call you "Sunshine" or something even more *southern*. She will give you a smile, make you laugh, and give you a big ol' Texas-sized hug. But if she starts talkin' really southern to you, this is not a good thing. When she says things like, "Bless your heart," it means that she is probably thinking, *this one is a real dingbat.* (Just warning you)!

Denise is the person everyone asks to speak when they need things to be funny. Like Lucy, she has red hair and just her facial expressions can make you roll on the floor laughing; she doesn't have to say a word. The girl has more biological malfunctions than Janet Jackson at the Super Bowl, though hers aren't planned. If she were to get another job, she could be a spokesperson for Depends. She is not limited in her gifts, however. She could also work for Ah Bra, Spanx, or anything else that constricts, rolls, slides, or goes south.

Denise's sense of humor is always at her own expense. She is the funniest accountant I have ever met. She is one of the few people I have known who actually uses both sides of her brain and can switch mid-thought like the flip of a dime. She likes dimes and anything dealing with specific numbers. I, on the other hand, am not much of a numbers person, preferring in most situations to round everything. Accountants really hate this, I might add.

When I moved to the desert, I lived so near the US border that when I went to the mall my cell phone said, "Welcome to Mexico." I was beyond culture shocked, and it wasn't even 117 degrees yet. (I said *yet*—wait for it!) Then I met this redhead, who was as friendly as could be, and I found myself thinking, *did I grow up with her in Illinois?* She is like the girl next door, or the sister you haven't met.

One night I was sitting in a women's Bible study with a large group of women I hardly knew. Denise just turned around and smiled at me, and for the first time I felt like I might be home after all.

Much later she told me that she had prayed for me. I thought she meant she had prayed for me as her pastor's wife, but she was talking about praying that God would send her a friend who turned out to be me. Oh, what joy there is in being treated like a normal person, to be called by name, to just be who you are and never be placed on a pedestal! And, by the way, Denise is far from perfect. After all, she is from Texas (a state of no pretense)! She is as real as the day is long, and that is pretty refreshing for someone who has lived in a glass house most of her life.

The sad thing is I almost missed having the kind of friendship we share. If Denise had let it go, we might have just stayed surface acquaintances forever. A year or two went by and I had completely missed the message that she had prayed for me to be her friend. I was heading out of town for a couple of weeks on a family vacation and she said, "I will miss you. Text me while you are gone." That was the day we first started writing our book, we just didn't know it yet.

As you read Denise's funny experiences you will realize what I mean. She talks openly and unashamedly about the things that most of us try to hide or forget. She will make you laugh until you cry. You may even think to yourself, *I can relate, and maybe it's OK to be just who I am... bodily functions, mishaps, and all.* Whether she is talking or writing, it is LOL funny!

Some are quick to stereotype funny people. They think they are always "up," that they don't have problems like others, or that they are less spiritual than "serious" Christians or Biblical students who would rather be curled up with their concordances. Some even think funny people are shallow and self-centered. I have found Denise to be way more complex than any stereotype, and I feel sorry for those who so easily judge others by their surface characteristics and miss such a treasure of friendship.

I am incredibly privileged to write this book with my dear friend, Denise. I have laughed harder, learned more about grace and acceptance, and have lived more fully the life that God intended since I have met this wacky, wonderful friend. Every pastor's wife needs a "Denise".

One of my all-time favorite memories of Denise is the day she got stuck in her tube in the lazy river. You see, when I first got to know her, she told me she had almost drowned as a child and had a crippling fear of water. I told her she needed to learn to enjoy being in and around water because I love it. My brilliant idea for healing her fear was, of course, the lazy river. Oh yeah, baby! We were going to float, drink some cold fruity drinks, and let all of life's troubles just melt away. We talked, laughed, relaxed, and floated.

Although she might not have admitted it, I think she had a pretty great time. Yes, it all went pretty well UNTIL she needed to get her 'tushy' out of the tube and back on dry land. The more she tried to get out of that tube, the deeper she sunk. So, being the good friend that I am, I tried to push from the back. She described the entire scene as feeling like an upside down turtle that got stuck in its shell.

I started out trying to be helpful, but the entire scene was a lot like one of the best moments from Lucy and Ethel's many adventures. You have to keep in mind that Denise is about six foot tall, so there were arms and legs going everywhere. Before long, I was cackling (as my teenage son likes to put it), then snorting, and then came the hiccups. With all of her body parts flailing, it was hard to breathe for all the laughing. And, to top it all off, a good friend of hers was standing up at the lazy river's entrance waiting for her and watching all of this.

That day Denise gained a few new memories connected to water although I can't say that her big water phobia went away completely. She is a good sport and is always willing to go float the lazy river with me, as I must admit there is never a dull moment.

Now you know how we discovered *Tubular Therapy* for the soul. We float, we talk, and we laugh. Fears become smaller, cares become lighter, and hope becomes brighter.

I look at it like this: if I could get Denise "with her death grip" crammed in a floaty little tube, I can get you into this ol' lazy river, too. So, grab a tube and bring your fruity drink along; the water feels just right. Let's float awhile and talk awhile. We'll laugh awhile and maybe even cry awhile. If you get stuck, I'll give you a little push. It might not be pretty, but it will be effective. We'll all go home feeling stronger than when we came.

What is *Tubular Therapy*? It is our journey of finding freedom and healing through friendship with God and His people. God's unconditional love sets us free from the fears that bind us.

Proverbs 27:17 (NIV) says, "As iron sharpens iron, so one person sharpens another." Other versions say that this sharpening involves the countenance of the friend's face. This book is written to put a smile on your face, and when you put it down it is our prayer that you will invest in the lives of friends by putting a smile on their face and growing in the joy of the Lord. *Tubular Therapy* is the story of "iron sharpening iron". Together we laugh. We grow. Our hope is renewed and strengthened through friendship and faith.

Tubular Therapy Thought

Everyone gets their "tushy" stuck in "the tube" sometime! When you feel stuck will you have a friend to lift you up?

CHAPTER TWO

Tubular Therapy

(Denise needs a little help with her "tushy" and "tube"
combination, but the truth is, we all need a little help
at times with our fears, friendships, and faith.)

"A cheerful heart is good medicine,
But a broken spirit saps a person's strength."
(Proverbs 17:22 NLT)

Funny Denise ...

For months Debbie and I had planned a getaway to finish writing this book. We had hotel reservations, massages scheduled, lazy rivers lined up, and restaurants to try. We paired it with the Anaheim Women of Faith conference and decided to stretch a three day conference into a five day weekend. But as life would have it, things didn't exactly go as planned.

Debbie found out on Wednesday that she was going to need a medical procedure on her arm and couldn't get the stitches wet for three days. The doctor assured her that her pain meds would do the trick, but she soon discovered that wasn't remotely close to handling the pain. The day we left, Debbie came down with a cold that quickly went south into her chest and the words "hacking up a lung" became synonymous with her name.

Her luggage went from being packed with shorts, swimsuits, beach towels and suntan lotion to night time sleep medicine, menthol rub, cling wrap, and boxes of tissues. Debbie has always been musical, so she adapted her shower routine accordingly, "You put your left arm in; you hang your right arm out." She felt pretty hokey with her cling wrap on and she was kind of pokey getting ready.

It was the final leg of our trip and we had reserved a room at a nice hotel on the way home. The room and bathroom were larger than expected and everything seemed fabulous. Being a bathroom connoisseur, I surveyed the oversized glass shower with appreciation, but then noticed the back wall of the shower was an enormous floor-to-ceiling window which provided a completely unobstructed view from the bedroom into the shower.

Now, this is a high class hotel so I thought, *OK ... a couple of things.*

First, there are trees with no leaves painted on this window, so maybe when the shower steams up these branches will sprout leaves to cover up the naked view. Second, maybe it's a window that fogs up when the shower is on to obstruct the view from the bedroom into the shower. Third, maybe it was an optical illusion for the sake of decoration.

Finally, an awful thought went through my mind, *what kind of a "special" suite was this, anyway?* So I stepped into the shower and called to Debbie who was on the other side of the window lying on her bed with her jumbo box of tissues.

"You can't see me right?"

"Oh my word...," she said, "YES, I CAN!!"

"Nooooo!"

"YESSSSS!!" she said again.

"Well maybe it will fog up when you take a shower and you can't see anything."

"You better hope it fogs up!" she shot back.

The next morning Debbie and I decided to check out the lazy river. We had until noon before we needed to check-out, so off we went to the pool. Our float was glorious and we finally came up with the title to our book. Feeling happy with the success of our float and all we had accomplished while relaxing at the same time, we reluctantly departed the lazy river knowing our morning was drawing to a close.

On returning to our room in our wet swimsuits, our key didn't work. At this point we only had 25 minutes to check out of our room, so we sent word to security to bring us another key. The poor security guard came twice to unlock our room with no luck.

So, there Debbie and I sat in our wet swimsuits in the hallway, her hacking up a lung and sending me to get tissues from the cleaning ladies, who left the box and quickly disappeared as soon as they heard Debbie's enormous cough. It soon became apparent that I had "issues" of my own. I greatly needed the "facilities" as my grandma liked to say, and I needed them sooner rather than later. However, I didn't think I could make it all the way down that long hallway to find a bathroom, even if there was one on that floor. Oh well, it was too late now and I figured if the situation became too dire I could always blame what was about to happen on my wet suit.

Finally, a repair guy and a security guard moseyed on down the hall like they had no place to be; they were obviously not in any hurry to get there. Six keys and over an hour later, we were still watching a parade of men come and go through our little hallway while sitting there in our wet swimsuits ... Debbie barking like a seal, and me needing to pee like a racehorse. Our little circus was becoming quite comical.

They tried different keys, new sensor chips – everything but a ramming device and a crow bar. By the time the man finally rebooted the sensor and let us in, we were beyond grins and giggles.

We were given a late check-out, an hour of laughter therapy, and another reminder that life is often shaped in those awkward, unexpected, (sometimes) humorous moments when our patience is tried, our friendship is deepened, and our soul has floated through another storm successfully.

Back in our room - which we referred to as the Peek-A-Boo Suite - we discussed how much we liked the water park and how much fun it would be to come back with our families someday, but we also wondered how we could ever bring our sons to this place if all the rooms were equipped with this one-of-a-kind shower.

You can imagine my surprise when I heard the sound of running water. Debbie is a very private person, so I was rather taken aback to hear the shower turn on at all. I will tell you that you couldn't see body parts but it was hard to escape the moving silhouette shadows that looked like sign language covering the wall of the room. How does one hide from a dancing shadow?

A short while later she sashayed out of the bathroom with more information about her Peek-a-Boo shower. I said, "I was sitting here trying to write, but it was really hard to miss a moving silhouette dancing on the walls and ceiling! It looked like the interpretive arm dance on the opening of the Cosby show. I looked up and it scared me; this bathroom is truly an original. Who would have ever guessed they put showers in like this? All I can say is that some man came up with this room design!"

I began to explain to Debbie that my original thoughts were sooooo off! "The leaves did not sprout, no amount of steam helped, the window was not frosted, and believe you me, that window was no Picasso."

Debbie said, "Yep, that's why I wore my swimsuit."

We laughed and agreed this was NOT the location for a woman's retreat but it would be the perfect romantic location to take our husbands for an anniversary. Debbie then began to tell me all about how cool the shower actually was. She said, "You've gotta see this ..."

I said, "I don't know about seeing the shower as I am having a hard time recovering from the scary dancing shadows that splashed on the walls!"

She went on to tell me that the Peek-a-Boo bathroom has two shower heads in there. "It is like shooting at you from all directions!" she exclaimed. She went on to explain that with all the steam and showers shooting everywhere she couldn't read any of the names on the five little bottles in there so she just grabbed them all and took them in the shower.

I said, "What were in all the bottles?"

She replied, "I have no idea so I just used a little of everything ... Not only did I use shampoo and conditioner but I think there was body wash, lotion, and mouthwash. My hair is not only clean, tangle free, and soft to the touch, but it is minty fresh too!"

When I stopped laughing, I thought about it, *why wouldn't the girl who took a bath in a church baptistery in her swimsuit be willing to try out anything with water in it?*

You will find out a little later in this book how I really feel about showers, swirling water, and drains; then add a see-through, full-length window into my privacy?

Not this southern belle ... I avoided the Peek-A-Boo shower at all cost!

Just Debbie ...

Our little trip is pretty typical of our lives. Just when we are ready to relax, regroup, and recharge we need to reboot our sensors, instead. Most of us start life wearing rose colored glasses; our minds are filled with dreams about how wonderful life will be. Life is always a lot more colorful than that, isn't it? We just know that our husbands will rise up and call us "blessed" like the Proverbs 31 woman. Our children will adore and praise us, our church will embrace us, and our emotional baskets will be filled with deep and rewarding friendships.

Then we enter the real world and see that the window into our little space is see-through and it is only when we are sitting out in the hall that the real adventure begins.

Perfect moments don't make perfect memories. Of all the memories we have in seeing this book come together, that hour long laughing session in the hallway will be at the top of the list. Next on the list are the Peek-A-Boo shower, and all of the times that we laughed as I wheezed and hacked up a lung. It was not perfect but it was certainly unpretentious.

Many of us have a crazy notion that we have to be perfect to come close to God. How could Jesus ever put up with someone as imperfect as us? We are often afraid to let people see the 'real us' as well. We are afraid that they will judge us, not like us, or find us inadequate. So, we put on a little mask and that is all we will really let people see of us.

Have you ever wondered if God even cares if you have a friend? What about the Son of God; since He was perfect did Jesus even need a friend or care if He had friends?

The Gospel of John gives us a little "close-up" look at the relationships of Jesus. John 15 records with unbiased honesty the words of Jesus to His closest followers, His disciples. We see that even on their best days they were easily distracted. Their pride, selfishness, and lack of faith often stood in the way of their love for God, and the people around them. They were very ordinary, rough, unpolished men. There was nothing pretentious about them ... nothing!

Judas betrayed his Master and Lord. Peter missed the message of servanthood and grabbed a sword to seek revenge. James and John, with their mother beside them, fought over who was the greatest in the kingdom of Heaven.

Let me ask you something, *would these ordinary, rough, unpolished men be the kind of friends for whom you would lay down your life?*

Please listen to the words that Jesus spoke to these very men. "You did not choose me, but I chose you. I have called you **friends**" (John 15: 15-16 NIV).

Many of us today do not begin to understand the Greek language. It is truly "Greek to us" and so we are missing some important thoughts about friendship that Jesus was sharing with his disciples.

In the Greek, the word for friend, *Philos*, comes from a common verb for love, *Phileo*. In the New Testament a "friend" is immediately understood as *one who loves*. Friendship was a key relationship in the ancient world. It was considered the glue that binds a free person to one another and their community. A friend was defined as *someone who would sacrifice their lives for one another and for the common good*.

When Jesus called these ordinary, imperfect men "friends" he was not just speaking flattery to them. He was saying to them, "I love you with a sacrificial love in which I am willing to lay down my own life."

What would Jesus think of *Tubular Therapy*? Each and every day He is the one that practiced it, modeled it, and demonstrated a "friendship kind of love" for us to follow. Many of Jesus' greatest lessons came to life while they floated on the seas together. During the greatest storms of life Jesus was there.

Perhaps you have heard the saying, "When the going gets tough, the tough get going." When life gets tough, it is time for some going, growing, and glowing. As we simply put one foot in front of the other, stepping out in faith like the disciples, we will grow in our relationship with God and others. The people around us will see His light shining though our lives in spite of our hard times. Much like that "Peek-A-Boo" window, there is no hiding from God's light.

Whether you are floating on a lazy river, walking down a rustic path, or sitting at a Starbucks sipping a green tea, your life can be so much better when God gives you a friend who is like a sister. Therapy is simply one friend talking to another and inviting God in. The first step on our journey is merely to let God's light shine in and allow our sisters in the family of God to minister to our broken, hidden places. Let's start by talking about some of those infamous fears. We all have them. Some are small. Some are big. Some are HUGE...and some are downright debilitating. They hold us back. They keep us in hiding and lonely. Don't feel alone! We understand exactly how it feels.

There are heights, planes, bad haircuts, dogs, rainy mountain roads, and much more!

Tubular Therapy Thought

Like the shadows from the "Peek-a-boo shower", there is no hiding from our fears. They will only grow bigger as they dance on the walls of our mind. God's plan for freedom from fear is unconditional love.

CHAPTER THREE
Mr. Drain-O-No!

*(There is nothing worse than spiders in
your shower . . . just ask Debbie.)*

*"Are not two sparrows sold for a penny? Yet not one of them
will fall to the ground outside your Father's care. So don't be
afraid. You are worth much more than sparrows."*
(Matthew 10:29, 31 The Message)

Funny Denise

The only drawback to floating down life's lazy river in my mind is the water...lots of water. The tube floats on water, the water goes up and down, splashes in your face, and can cover your head. That, my friends, is a definite drawback to floating. I have enough trouble just dealing with water in my very own bathroom. My problem started when I was very young.

My biggest fear as a child was not snakes or heights. It was the SHOWER – specifically, the DRAIN in the shower. To look at me now you wouldn't believe it, but I was a very skinny child. We moved to a rental house outside of Memphis, Tennessee while our new house was being built. The rental house was missing a vital part of my life: a bathtub. All that was in this house was a shower, a small square box with a shower curtain about three feet across. The shower wasn't the worst of it. The drain was my issue.

There was no drain cover in this particular shower and the drain had a hole the size of TEXAS! I remember the first time I looked in there and thought to myself, *there is no way I can take a shower in there. I am afraid of water and now not only is the water going to be coming down over my head to drown me, but I am going to slip quietly down that drain and NOBODY will ever find me. I will be the disappearing little girl who went to take a shower and never came back out ... neither clean nor dirty ... just missing.*

The first day we lived there I told my mom I had a cold and I couldn't take a shower as I didn't feel well. That lie worked for two days until I couldn't fake a sneeze. The third day I told her that I tried to take a shower and there was no hot water so I would just take it the next day and quickly ran off to bed. The fourth day I was busted. Mom escorted me into the bathroom and opened the shower curtain, turned on the water and said, "OK, now you march your little self in there and take a shower like a big girl." The problem was I wasn't a big girl. I was seven... and I was scared!

She left the bathroom and there I sat with a towel wrapped around me, crying. I heard a knock on the door and there was my savior, my daddy. He loved me! He would save me! He wouldn't make me EVER take ANOTHER shower again! I remember he squatted down in front of me and said, "Denny ... what's the matter?" I said, "Daddy ... I don't like the water in the shower hitting my face and now there is a big hole in the floor where the water goes down and if I misstep I am gone forever down that drain!"

He smiled, hid his laughter and said, "Look ... it will be OK. Get in the shower and I will help you." I stepped in the shower, closed the curtain, handed him the towel and he took my hand. He held my hand the entire time I was in that shower and told me if I slipped down that drain and was washing away to the great never-never land of shower water, he would pull me back up. I had nothing to fear.

I am over 50 years old now and every time I step into a shower and am worried about anything for that day, I think of my daddy holding my hand, ready to pull me out whenever I feel like I am being washed down the drain. Isn't God that way, too?

All we have to do is ask and God is there to give us a hand to keep us from going down life's drain, just like my daddy!

Just Debbie...

Unlike Denise, I am not so much afraid of what can go down a drain as what can come up out of the drain. You may recall the catchy little children's song, "The Itsy Bitsy Spider went UP the water spout." See, right there, the song actually says it! Besides, the hairy friend I encountered was not "itsy" and certainly not "bitsy." He was brown, large, and beefy.

I was sick, so I was staying in the downstairs guest bedroom next to a small bathroom. It was late at night and I had been awakened by nature's call. I stepped out of bed in my PJ's and bare feet and headed off to use the facilities. I was sitting there minding my own business, staring at my bare feet when I saw this brown, hairy body. It was big and quick and it scared the life right out of me! Suddenly, I was doing my very own version of a dance from the 1950s movie "The Music Man" called the "Shipoopi"!

The door was closed, my feet were bare, and it was on the move in my direction. Yep, I was freaking out! I started lifting my feet and grabbing weapons even though I was NOT dressed for battle. My "tunic" was down around my feet and I could not find my "shield of faith" anywhere. So, I grabbed a can of Lysol thinking, *I will stun it or make it smell like summer flowers, whichever comes first.*

I climbed on top of the toilet seat. There was no way I was coming down. If necessary, I would climb up on the sink. As a softball champion, the can became my bat and I was aiming for the outfield. I slammed the can of Lysol right down on top of this sucker. The crowd went wild. (WHAA...) Ok. Perhaps that wasn't the crowd; it was just me.

When I picked up the can, there was nothing under it. Nothing! How could that be? Did I disintegrate it? Where did it go? I looked all over the room, but it was nowhere to be found.

I was sick and stuck with my mighty cough downstairs in the guest room with only a door between me and the bathroom that the brown, hairy spider had now claimed as its little domain. This spider had invaded my special refuge of rest and recuperation. What was I to do? I was drugged with nighttime cold medicine, ready to conk out, and the spider was roaming freely wherever it pleased. This thought just grossed me out, so I used a towel to cover the crack underneath my door, but the bedroom was whispering its name ... oh yeah ... I could hear it! This had become a challenge between the two of us. I put my shoes on and climbed back in bed. The spider knew what my feet looked like ... fool me once, but not twice. I would be ready the next time!

Lying in my bed with the towel in front of my door, my shoes now on, and the covers pulled up tightly, I pondered this thought *how can I be brave?*

"Fear Not!" That's what the Bible teaches us, and yet we all have fears and phobias. Most phobias stem from something that happened in our lives when we were young that we just can't get past as adults, like Denise's fear of water.

Funny Denise...

My fear of the water is a result of almost drowning at Myrtle Beach, North Carolina as a young child. I was five years old, riding on my father's shoulders as he carried me out to the ocean. I remember the laughter and the waves hitting my feet as my dad walked farther and farther into the water. He turned around and was heading back to shore when a huge wave hit us from behind knocking him forward off his feet. I fell off his shoulders and into the water. He always had a solid hold on me, but I didn't realize it. I remember holding onto his legs and the ocean water swirling around us.

My eyes were burning and I was swallowing salt water. The churning surf was dragging me forward and backward under the water, tossing me around like a rag doll. This was likely no more than a few seconds, but for me it seemed like an eternity. The next thing I remember was lying on the beach choking up salt water.

From that brief period of just a few seconds under water, I developed a fear that caused me to never want to get in the ocean again. Even the smell of the ocean turns my stomach. This fear has transferred to pools and other bodies of water, as well.

Debbie, on the other hand, is a fish! Every place we go must have a fabulous pool, a lazy river, or a Jacuzzi made for the stars. If we go to a restaurant, it needs to be overlooking water, if at all possible. Her goal in life is to get me in the water whenever time or place allows.

We took a group of 12 women to a condo in Solano Beach, California last summer. While I admit that standing on the hill overlooking the ocean was gorgeous, the 150 steps down to the beach and back up was a nightmare. However, one morning at the crack of dawn, Debbie and I decided to get some exercise walking in the sand. It was a secluded part of the beach only open to people who were members or guests of the Solano Beach condo association. I was beginning to feel the relaxed attitude often associated with the California way of life and I decided to walk the beach in flannel pajama pants and a sweatshirt. It was a beautiful morning in November, so off we went down the 150 stairs to the beach.

We were told one significant fact by the owner when we left the condo ... which way to turn at the base of the stairs. This was important in order to avoid having to climb back up those stairs to get back to the condo. We were supposed to end our beach walk at the lifeguard station and then come back up the main road. When we got to the bottom of the stairs, I turned right and Debbie turned left. We stood at the base of the stairs and debated the issue. Directions are pretty important, so whatever possessed me to believe "directionally challenged Debbie" is beyond comprehension, but I did and we turned left.

The best part about our friendship is that no matter where we are and what we are doing, we are laughing and talking and having a great time, so we were really enjoying ourselves walking barefoot on the sand down the beach. Debbie has the gift of diversion; she is really good at it. She knows what worries me and tries to refocus my attention whenever she knows I will be stressed about something. However, this time it was not really working and the life guard station never appeared. High tide, however, was rapidly materializing as we walked. The water was slowly making its way onto the beach and I was running out of dry shore.

It seemed we walked for miles until we came to the last jut of rocks that we had to maneuver around. High tide had eaten up most of the beach by this point, so we had to time the waves to make it around the rocks without having to swim. I think I remember hearing screams (mine) as I ran around the rocks, but we finally made it to what they call Dog Beach.

I may not yet have explained that I don't exercise. My idea of exercise is rolling my chair from my desk to the fax machine and back. So, by the time we made it to Dog Beach, I was dog tired. We walked another few hundred miles - OK, maybe not, but it was FAR - before making it to the main road. Exhausted, I decided to call in reinforcements.

I called the owner of the condo and asked how far away we were. I should have known something was up when she said, "Well, you're just a couple of blocks from the condo ... well ... maybe a few blocks ... well, maybe we should come get you in the car."

In hindsight, I should have trusted the owner of the condo and sat down to wait, but oh no ... not Debbie! She said, "We aren't that far and we can make this walk. It'll be fine."

Now to put this into perspective, Solano Beach is like the Beverly Hills of San Diego. Here I was in pajamas, hair not combed, out of breath and *walking uphill* – another little fact that might have been good to know ahead of time - on the sidewalk along the main thoroughfare of Solano Beach. I think I've had dreams like this, but most people would call them nightmares.

It was chilly out that morning. I knew I was cold, but there was something else going on, something quite ... well ... breezy. We had changed directions to head back toward the condo, and now the wind was coming from behind us. That's when I began to notice a distinct draft lofting through the posterior region of my PJ's. Debbie had loaned me some of her extra pajamas as I had forgotten to pack mine for the trip. I stopped and asked Debbie, "Is there a HOLE in these PJ's, because my derrière needs some defrosting?"

She couldn't breathe from laughing so hard, so I doubt that she even looked to see, and if she had looked and *seen* a hole ... would she REALLY tell me??

We still laugh about that trip and the "holey" pajamas. Debbie's objective was to help me overcome my fear of the ocean by creating a new memory for me. I definitely gained a new memory of the ocean, but it did not exactly work out the way she had planned.

As Debbie mentioned earlier, I also have issues with "tushies" and "tubes". Another of Debbie's good intentions to teach me that the water is my friend happened one beautiful, sunny Saturday when we decided to take Debbie's daughter, Chelsea, to the lazy river and float all afternoon. I am pretty good at standing in waist high water, so we got inner tubes, put them over our heads and started to float.

We had been floating for a while when I noticed a lot of the people were sitting in their inner tubes. They had their nice little drinks and looked so cool and comfortable. I thought to myself, *I can do this! Somehow I can sit in that inner tube with my little virgin Piña Colada and just float.* So I took the inner tube off over my head and stood on the stairs thinking, *Just sit ... all you have to do is sit in this inner tube.* Now in my mind this scenario worked. On paper this scenario worked. But, by George, when you add up a lazy river, moving water, a slick inner tube, and a shaky Denise, you have all the ingredients for a massive disaster.

After several tries with Debbie hee-hawing from the sidelines, she finally decided it was time to help this ol' girl out. She grabbed the inner tube and held it steady, telling me, "Just sit. Just Sit. JUST SIT!"

So I closed my eyes, grabbed ahold of the inner tube, and PLOP! Oh baby! I was in! I was completely jazzed to be seated comfortably in the water. I had my drink in one hand and the sun in my face. I was in "high cotton" as my daddy would say. We floated for what seemed like an hour and I was laughing and having a grand old time ... until I realized that the longer I floated, the farther I was sinking into the tube. There was more of me under the water than there was sitting above it, and soon panic set in as my fear of going completely under the water grew. The lazy river was becoming increasingly more crowded, but I knew I couldn't get out of this tube without making a fool of myself.

As I floated around the last time, I told Debbie I needed to get out because one of my other friends was waiting for me up at the entrance.

"I'll help you get out. Just stop at the stairs, *it's easy!*" Those were Debbie's famous last words!

She didn't realize I felt and looked like a turtle upside down in its shell, and the shell wasn't coming loose. We got to the stairs and Debbie said, "Lean over and put your feet on the stairs." ... easier said than done.

I couldn't get my legs out, and the harder I tried, the more SUCTION there seemed to be between the tube and my posterior. A small crowd of onlookers was gathering as Debbie's antics to get me out of the tube weren't exactly working. Finally, she just tipped me over and out I flopped ... flailing arms, legs, and all!

Just Debbie...

Most of us want our faith to keep us afloat like a big ol' inner tube, but we really don't like getting into the rough waters that cause our faith to grow. Sometimes we flop and flail much like Denise did trying to get out that day, when it would be better to just sit in our faith and trust. We prefer our easy chairs to facing our fears. Our journey through life is no different than floating down the river. Sometimes there is an undertow, and WATER ... lots of blue rushing water.

Hey, maybe floating and going for a walk is not such a bad idea after all. No wonder the apostle Peter asked Jesus if he could walk with Him on the water. They had just come through a big storm and he was sitting there in his fears. He needed to walk through his fears in order to touch a faith that could help him stand. With each step he took, he was closer to the hands that could steady him. The question is, "Are we walking close to the hand that can catch us?"

I know a little bit about how Denise feels about swirling water. Water relaxes me, but the mere thought of dogs and doctors sends me over the edge. My first memory of life at age three was being attacked by a dog that I tried to pet while it was eating. (Since then, I have learned some people are like that too, but that is a story for another time.) I tried to pet the dog and it attacked my face. I had lots and lots of stitches; many were right by my eye. I am very fortunate that I did not lose my eyesight.

I remember two very important things about that day. First they did not use Novocain to stitch up my face, and second, my dad was not able to be there with me. I was a little child, all alone in that room full of scary medical people. Unfortunately, my dad had to go perform a wedding while all of this was happening to me. All-in-all, it was pretty traumatic, and thus began my long history of fearing hospitals.

At the age of five, I was hospitalized with Pneumonia. I lived in my own little oxygen tent for a week. Every day they would take me, by myself, down to the hospital basement to lie unclothed under a sun lamp. I felt abandoned and vulnerable. This large room was their break room where the male orderlies and nuns laughed, played cards and smoked cigarettes ... while I lay under the sunlamp being treated for Pneumonia! (I know this seems unbelievable!)

After one of these treatments, I came back to my room to find my dad waiting for me. As I was only five years old, he was rather surprised to find me with packs of cigarettes. I proudly explained to him how they got in my room. I was tired of the nuns and orderlies smoking while I had these treatments, so I had gathered up their cigarette packs and stuck them in my PJ's. Yep, the problem was solved! It is amazing how we learn wrong coping behaviors to deal with fear, often starting when we are very young.

I may have gone home cured of pneumonia, but my heart had already begun a lifetime of fear. My first memory is of needles, pushing in and out of the skin by my eye. It is no wonder I decided at a very early age that all doctors and anything related to a hospital was to be avoided at ALL cost! The problem with our fears is that they grow over time.

When my little boy was about 3 three years old, I learned to conquer some of my own fears. This perfectly healthy, active little boy woke up ashen-faced one morning and could hardly breathe. I scooped him up and headed to our doctor's office, pronto! They worked on him for a long time and then called an ambulance to take him to the hospital. This was the only time I have ever seen an ambulance with sirens blaring, pull over to the side of a freeway so the mother could jump out of the front seat and climb in the back. As I rode in the ambulance that day, I heard these melodic words over and over in my head, "You are awesome in this place, mighty God. You are awesome in this place, Abba Father." Without explanation, I was overcome with a peace beyond understanding which guarded my previously fearful heart and mind.

God gave us a wonderful, caring Christian doctor who would help us understand how to care for a little boy with asthma and an extreme allergy to animals of all types and sizes.

Years later I would ask my son, "What do you remember about your time in the hospital?" You would have thought we had spent a week's vacation at Disneyland! He remembered us watching movies together, getting snacks, going to the craft room, and walking the hall together. He wore these little flounder slippers that were as big as he was, and the sight of him walking the halls in those slippers produced smiles and chuckles from all the people that saw him. He remembered my family bringing toys, and my good friend, Christine, bringing us burgers; it was like an upscale picnic. His funny version of his hospital stay made my heart glad. I stayed with my little boy day and night. I knew I could not take away his pain from the shots and treatments, but I could be with him. We actually had a lot of fun together in spite of everything.

You know, our Father God is like that. He does not take our pain away, although He could, and we wish He would. We live in a fallen world with consequences from sin. That is much like my son living in a world where he is allergic to animals.

God is always there with us. He is the security, love, and peace that fill the room so we are never alone. He is the Daddy who holds our hand in the showers of life.

I have come to understand that anyone who has experienced loss or pain through separation, trauma, divorce, or death often has trouble trusting God or other people in their lives. We tend to get stuck where we have been hurt. We wonder *where God is when we really need him.*

The most prominent and powerful words that the angels spoke throughout the entire Bible were "Fear Not!" When Mary found out she was pregnant, she had to be afraid. She wasn't even legally married to Joseph yet. How was she going to explain it? I find it very interesting that God directed her to go stay with Elizabeth who was also having a child that would be used by God. They went through their challenging time together.

Many of us try to hide our fears and figure out solutions by ourselves. Some of us just go ahead and steal the cigarettes. This is the do it yourself, hands-on, fix-it approach. Other times we analyze, withdraw, and try to keep our fears to ourselves.

The word "Emmanuel" means "God with us" and was the name given to Jesus. Isn't it amazing that God would take on flesh to be with us? God's answer to our fears is His presence, His people, and His peace.

Franklin D. Roosevelt told us, "The only thing we have to fear is fear itself!" This man knew personally what it was like to face a crippling disease. You see, fear becomes debilitating because it quenches our faith. God's message over and over in the Bible was simply, "Fear Not! Put your faith in me."

Many of us are emotionally stuck at the age where our greatest fear occurred and it is as real to us today as it was back then even though we are no longer helpless children. When we walk into a similar situation as adults, we now have the ability to cope with things differently than we did when we were young. We need to be willing to try.

Making a new memory to replace a bad old memory is a great start. God's prescription for our fears is to hold a hand, be a friend, share a smile, and connect. The death of fear starts with our very first step of faith. Ralph Waldo Emerson put it this way, "When we do the thing we fear, the death of fear is certain."

When God asks you to walk through something, you can walk in faith, not fear, knowing He is with you. I love to read Hebrews 11 because each story begins with the words, "By faith ..." Faith is the opposite of fear. We cannot sit in fear and go with God. All of the people in Hebrews 11 were just ordinary, fallen individuals who took a big God at His Word. If God says to build it, we should build it. Remember ... with God's help, amateurs built the Ark. Professionals built the Titanic.

Matthew 8:26 NIV says, "He replied, 'you of little faith, why are you so afraid?' Then he got up and rebuked the winds and the wave and it was completely calm." Isn't it time that we take our fears to the one that calms the winds and waves of our lives with just His words alone?

Drains, spiders, and doctors too ... what's a girl to do? I bet you have some fears of your very own.

Isn't it time we all just let those big, bad fears slide right on down old Mr. Drain?

Tubular Therapy Thought

God's answer to our fears is His presence, His people, and His peace. When you are most afraid, look up, reach out, and find a hand to hold. Take a step in faith and watch fear flee.

CHAPTER FOUR

BFF's

Debbie (left) & Denise (Right)—Denise truly needs a little help with water and inner tubes. Debbie needs help with directions, numbers, and other things. We all need a hand up at times ...

"If one person falls the other can reach out and help. But someone who falls alone is in real trouble."
(Ecclesiastes 4: 10 NLT)

Funny Denise...

Drains, dogs, heights, doctors ... do any of those words bring fear to your heart? What about the word, ALONE? Do you ever fear being abandoned, forgotten, or rejected? I grew up in more cities than I can count, and I know what it feels like to be the "new kid". I also know what it is like to look around and think that everyone has already established their group of friends.

If we are to be honest and face our fears as we set out on this journey we must be honest to say that many of us are afraid of people, not just things. We are afraid that people won't like us, we don't fit in, and that someone will hurt us if we ever reach out our hand in friendship. The problem with these fears is that they keep us lonely, very lonely.

You know how all your life you pray for that "soul sister" kind of friend? Somehow you are on the same wave-length and she just "gets you" and has what you are lacking. You find yourself a better person because of your friendship, and you are always stronger just because she is in your life. I met her almost 4 years ago. It was wintertime in the desert and the winds were whipping me, inside and out.

I always wondered what the definition of a best friend was and just exactly what that friendship would look like. Most people believe friendship is made up of laughing and enjoying each other's company. I now know that is the fluff, or the icing, on the friendship. A true friendship is forged during those times in your life when you have sadness, anger, frustration, worry, and all the other emotions that show up when you aren't at your best. Can you imagine going through life and only having a best friend when times are good, but being alone when times are rough? I would like to say that our friendship started on an equal footing, but I would be sorely mistaken, as she has reminded me over the years.

Perhaps you, too, have experienced the winter of your soul. For me, winter had moved in and taken up residence. I was in a pretty dark place for a few years before I met Debbie. I had pulled away from being a youth sponsor for the high school kids and wasn't really involved in much at church. I would show up on Sunday mornings, paste on my normal smile, and give my typical answers. "How are you...I am fine." Then I would head home from church, no one the wiser. My life had taken a turn for the worse with a lot of decisions that had led me to start my own business. It was a scary decision, but seemed to be my only choice at the time. I needed to make this work. I forgot about everything I enjoyed, and church was part of that.

In July we got hit with the news that our pastor was moving to Indiana and we would, once again, be looking for another one. I thought to myself, *not again! It's so hard to keep coming to church without a good pastor; and pretending to be nice to all the candidates is just exhausting.*

About that same time, my mom moved back to Texas, and a good friend of mine had also moved away. My life seemed full of loss. I felt like I was traveling down an unfamiliar road, not knowing where I was going. Finally, I did what I should have been doing all along. I began to pray for a friend. Not just any friend ... I had plenty of friends in my life. I wanted a best friend; the one you can tell anything to and know that they have your back, no matter what.

I needed somebody to get me back on the right road, the road leading back to church, the road that was going to give my life purpose again. I needed the kind of friend that only God could give me if I humbly asked.

At the same time, Debbie was praying too. But she was praying NOT to come to our church. She didn't want to live in the desert and she *really* didn't want to move from her home in Missouri. I was praying harder, apparently, because my prayers were answered. Debbie and her family moved to Southern California in January the following year. I first met her at a women's brunch I attended with my mom.

Please understand that I am not putting her down when I say she is NOT the stereotypical preacher's wife. She can act the part, but the real Debbie is far from that.

She was speaking that day and all was going well when, all of a sudden, she said, "I want you to know something about me ..." She proceeded to tell the "bubble bath in the baptistery story". I couldn't stop laughing and realized that she had a quirky way about her that perfectly matched my personality as I am pretty quirky most of the time, too.

I felt a friendship with her that clicked immediately. The only issue was I didn't think she felt that instant friendship with me; at least, she didn't appear to be aware of it. While I felt like we were BFFs, Debbie had grown up as a preacher's kid, "PK", and had learned early in life to keep her guard up. We talked about everything and laughed about most things. All in all, she would laugh at the things I would share, but she was actually sharing very little about herself.

I was on the Women's Ministry team with her and we traveled to many different places together. After about a year, Debbie told me she wanted to have a Women's Conference at a resort out of town and wanted me to go check it out with her. The resort was beautiful but the next day we got word that her dad had a stroke and had been taken to the hospital. Up until this point in our friendship we were just surface friends talking about those safe, surface things that make you laugh. This was a turning point in our friendship. This was where the rubber met the road.

Questions were running through my mind as we drove to Orange County: *How do you take care of someone that is going through something this emotional? What do you say? What do you do for them?*

I didn't have any answers, but God did. He told me to just be there for her ... that's all. Just be there. No special words of wisdom, no special gifts. Just be there ... that's it. I remember asking God, "Are you sure? I mean, I can tell jokes, I can make her laugh, I can buy junk food, get her favorite bagel ..." But God said, "No ... just be there. That's it."

So, for a whole weekend I sat with her in the hospital, in the corner, in a chair, with a blanket. I was there. I was there when she had tears. I was there when she couldn't make her dad understand. I was there when she put her head in her hands and didn't know what to do anymore. I was there.

The part that I didn't tell you is that we were not only checking out the resort, but Debbie was preparing for oral surgery scheduled for Monday morning to remove a tumor in her cheek. She was trying to stay cool, calm, and collected, but that pretty veneer went out the window when she got the news about her dad.

On Monday morning she had her surgery; then she wanted to go by and see her dad again before we headed back home. As she was sitting by her dad's bedside, he was very restless and confused which was hard for her to watch. She kept tapping my leg as if to say, *did you hear that? Are you paying attention here?* While she was in the midst of this she received a phone message that her daughter had been taken to the hospital with a gallbladder attack and to come home right away. That was the third strike, and she was OUT! Her head went in her hands and her mask came off.

It was a long, painful ride home for her, physically and emotionally. I handed her little pieces of scrambled eggs to eat. The events of that trip had cracked her façade and broken the ice. I knew God had allowed me to be there with her, but I just had no idea what twists and turns we would take along the way. God knows when delicate moments are headed our way before we do, and He is faithful to prepare us and give us the help we need.

You know how Ecclesiastes talks about how we all fall down and will need a hand up? Well, I am wondering, *do scrambled eggs count?*

I am amazed at how God prompts us so He can use us. He answers our prayers as we simply obey, even if it means just being there. Being obedient when I felt God wanted me to go on that trip, and then sitting in silence with her instead of acting on my own impulses, was a turning point. It was the moment in our friendship that God showed Debbie the one thing she most needed to know: I am her friend. I am not leaving. I will always be there. I saw something, too. I saw the vulnerable side of her that added another layer of depth to our friendship.

The greatest gift a friend can give to another friend is to walk with them through their fears even though they are also afraid. Debbie has done that for me. She has this tremendous fear of doctors … to the point of avoiding them for years!

I got sick and needed to have a procedure. After multiple doctor visits and a month or so of her prodding me to go, she pushed me to schedule it and off we went to the hospital. We talked while we sat in the waiting room, then she reluctantly went with me to the prep room before the procedure and kept me talking the whole time to distract me – well, probably to distract us both.

We even worked out a plan to exit the hospital and run like the wind to get out of there, but she stayed and talked me through the wait. When the nurse came in and asked if I was ready, I said, "Can she go with me … into the room for the procedure? Please???" The nurse said she didn't think that was allowed.

Debbie acted like she was disappointed, but told me that she would be waiting for me when I got out. She kept telling me that I wasn't going to be alone. It was comforting and reassuring. Then the nurse came back and gave me the greatest news ever. The doctor would allow Debbie to come in the room with me! I was so excited, but noticed she was pale.

As they rolled me into the procedure room, she said, "I will be right back."

I looked around and thought to myself, *she is going to bolt out the exit door and run like the wind!* But moments later I saw the green shirt.

There she was, touching my foot and letting me know that she was there and she wasn't going anywhere.

To put this into perspective, Debbie passes out at the sight of blood. So, for her to just be there was a huge step. But isn't that what being a BFF is all about?

Just Debbie...

I first heard the term, "BFF" a couple of years ago. One of the high school girls said to me, "Where is your BFF?"

I said, "My what?"

"You know! The funny red head that makes you laugh!"

I went home and asked my high school age son, "What is a BFF?" He kindly explained this new term to me. You know, high school kids today are pretty sharp. They can sense joy and friendship when they see it, and I think their terminology is right on track with what God has in mind for our relationships in the body of Christ, as well; these relationships are eternal investments. As for the term BFF ... it has stuck with us ever since.

I have truly been blessed with friendships that are like my own flesh and blood sisters. Many years ago a group of girlfriends from church had planned a wonderful birthday surprise for one of our dear friends. One of the gals in the group rented a limousine to pick us all up so we would enjoy a scenic drive, wonderful appetizers, and end up at a nice restaurant by the beach to celebrate our friend's big birthday. I had really looked forward to this for a while as I love this group of gals - they are just so much fun – and this would be my very first limo ride. How exciting! I could not wait!

The day of the big event came and I got all dressed up in my black outfit ... smellin' good, lookin' good ... I was ready to roll! On my way out, I stopped to give my little boy a hug and kiss. As I bent down, he sat up; out came his dinner with the force of a mighty wave. I was stunned! Did this darling little boy just assault me with the full force of a Public Works Department? My stylish black outfit was no longer black, and I no longer looked or smelled good.

The interesting thing is that the limo instantly lost its glamour; the fun night out with the girls lost its appeal. All that mattered to me was sitting with this sweet little boy of mine. I had lost all desire to leave him for a big evening out. Like that night, our friends can sometimes take second place at an inopportune time. In fact, we are never the center of our friend's world. We are simply there to come alongside them and be their friend. We are to point them to God first and help them keep their priorities in line. This book is about friendship, and the most important thing I can tell you about a true friend is that they are there in the good times and bad.

Many ladies have told me that they don't have a close friend because someone, at some time, has let them down. I almost missed getting to know Denise for that very reason. It is hard to make friendships in the church when you are a pastor's wife, and it is much harder after you have been burned. The truth, however, is that we are all human and every one of us is going to blow it at some time, and in some way. We can never fill someone's empty spaces either. Only God can do that. We can give each other the grace to make mistakes, and provide encouragement in good times and bad. When that is not enough, we can forgive.

To any of you who have experienced heartbreak through a friendship, I understand that part, as well. My husband and I have been blessed with a lifetime of rich friendships and amazing ministries. However, it only takes one heartbreaking church situation to burst your bubble and break your heart.

I met Denise after a church situation which was exactly that. I wasn't looking for any friends. I was just recovering. My tube was not quite afloat. I truly DID feel an instant kinship with her, I just wasn't sure I ever wanted a close friend in the church again.

Like Moses, God called me to "wander in the wilderness" for an overhaul of my broken spirit (i.e. move to the desert). I had no sense of humor ... zero, zip, nada! God has got to be the master designer of all humor, as He sent Denise in my direction. She was wackier than all of my past friends put together and multiplied by 10! She was also accepting, encouraging, and non-judgmental.

I guess my dad was right after all. He said, "It's the people that make the town, not the landscape." The church God has placed me in is filled with loving people. They are simply the best of the best. The tapestry of my life is being filled once again with the beauty and light of friendships. Sometimes God does not give you what you ask for; instead He gives you what you truly need and you are so much better because of His intervention in your life.

People stuck in addictions, broken homes, and anger will tell you that they feel alone. Most of these people do not feel that they have a friend in the world. They feel isolated, and they are seeking comfort in a chosen companion that is not good for them and can, in some cases, destroy their lives.

One of the most troubling things in our society today is the increase in school massacres by troubled young people. Many of the perpetrators of these horrendous acts of violence did not even know most of their victims. Some interesting characteristics that link these troubled, violent killers are that most of them were loners, who felt unloved, picked on or bullied, not accepted by anyone, and were often involved in a fantasy world of violent video games and internet applications. They had become filled with hate and vengeance. They were not relating with real people or receiving real love from anyone. People who hurt others are most often people that have been hurt themselves. The problem is that they are stuck in a dark pit of un-forgiveness ... a lonely, isolating, destructive place to live.

How is it that people can sit in church Sunday after Sunday and hear sermon after sermon, and then just walk away into a life of sin? Many have heard the Word, but they were unable or unwilling to accept it and apply it to their own lives. Perhaps they never let anyone get close enough to share their struggles. If we are unwilling to let people get close to us, we can miss God's greatest healing in our lives. We live in the Age of Information. There is better technology, more therapists, and more modes of communication than there has ever been in the history of the world. Yet, people are lonelier than ever. Have you ever wondered why?

Our family loves to watch old TV series like "Little House on the Prairie" and "The Waltons." These folks had one community, one church, one little store, and one place where they all gathered to talk and eat. They had one doctor who came to their house and the town's people brought them homemade food when they were sick. Life was not perfect; it was unpretentious. It was about community, not glamour. It was about friendship, not possessions.

The Bible gives us a glimpse of the friendship between David and Jonathan. They loved each other like brothers. Jonathan was not the center of David's world; rather, he was a support in everything he did. Jonathan loved David like a brother and he was willing to lay down his life for his friend. After Jonathan's death, David fell into sin. David really lost his way for a while. He walked into an affair and even had the woman's husband killed. This man after God's own heart really lost his footing after he lost his friend. We can lose our way, too, when we don't have a solid friend in our life.

When we read stories of the great people of faith in the Bible, we see that they rarely succeeded alone. God sent the apostles out two by two. When Elijah was discouraged, God gave him a protégée named Elisha. When Moses was tired, He sent his brother Aaron to hold up his arms. When Mary was pregnant and felt very much alone as Joseph was privately thinking of quietly putting her away, she went to spend time with Elizabeth.

As females, we need mothers, sisters, friends, and mentors in the faith. The Bible clearly tells us that the older women need to teach the younger women. We need a safe place to share, learn, and grow. These women nurture us, befriend us, remind us to sit at Jesus' feet, and serve us when we are in need. When we need God's touch, He sends a human hand. When we are burdened with cares, He sends us a smile. When we are overwhelmed with loss and grief, He sends us a comedian.

When we come to know God, He adopts us into His family, and His family is bigger than "My Big Fat Greek Wedding." Oompa!

The word "Oompa" in the Greek actually means "Yea!" or "Whoopee!" It is the essence of celebration, joy, togetherness, and life. This is the picture of what the church is supposed to be like. It is a family hooked together for life. We now have brothers, sisters, mothers, and fathers in the faith. I truly believe that God brings us different friends for the different seasons of our lives, but some friends are gifts for a lifetime. Like "My Big Fat Greek Wedding" they are those quirky relatives that bring the Windex to apply to "our zits and boo-boo's" when we need it. This extended family is larger than life to us.

A good friend is like a compass that helps you find your way when you can't tell which direction you should go, and a true friend provides a hand up when you have fallen down. As much as I hate the very thought of it, I must admit that life is a lot like bungee jumping. While we are trying to stay as far away from the edge as possible, we all need a rope tied around us, because there will come a day that the bottom just seems to drop right out from under us. On that day you will need a friend who is faithfully holding your rope.

We dare not go through life without opening up our hearts to the people that later on will become our very lifeline. I thank God for friends and mentors, who have prayed for me and provided encouragement, humor, and growth in my daily life. I am thankful for best friends through-out all the years of my life that have supplied an endless supply of "Windex" when I needed it the most.

Falling is inevitable. Receiving a hand-up is invaluable. The gift of friendship is simply priceless.

I don't want to miss the celebration and so I re-sound the word from my favorite movie, "Oompa!"

Tubular Therapy Thought

A true friend is a gift from God. They will encourage you to be all that God desires for you to be ... And they will bring the Windex!

CHAPTER FIVE
Free Falling

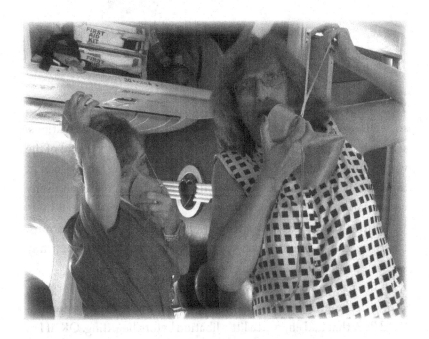

(Trying out the oxygen masks on our little flight to Vegas to see "The Lion King" ... Debbie is not a big fan of heights, sudden drops, and really doesn't care for these oxygen masks! Denise, however, is having a grand ol' time.)

"After Job prayed for his friends, the Lord restored his fortunes and gave him twice as much as he had before ... The Lord blessed the latter part of Job's life more than the former."
(Job 42:10, 12a NIV)

Funny Denise...

You know I just love the word, "Freeeeeeeeee! I'm Freeeeeeeeee!!" It's so, well, "Freeing" isn't it? There are no time constraints, limitations, schedules, or pressures choking me. I am NOT, however, fond of the word "falling". In fact, I wonder how the words "free falling" can fit together in the very same phrase. Those words are not even in my vocabulary!

With a father who was a trouble-shooter for large corporations, I have been flying since I was four years old. I've had a lot of funny excursions and a few terrifying ones.

One particular time, I was on a flight from Dallas to Hartford, sitting in the middle seat. My flight companions included a jumbo-sized flyer that had enjoyed a little libation before boarding. OK, if I'm being honest, he was sloshed. We can call him Mr. Abundance-in-All-Things, or Mr. Abundance, for short. On the other side of me was a sweet older lady who happened to be a nun. Her name, of course, was Mary. I thought of the old show "The Flying Nun" and chuckled to myself thinking I had my very own version sitting right next to me. It was Christmas time and I couldn't wait to get home. I had been away at college, finals were over, and I just needed some rest and relaxation.

We were fifteen minutes outside of Chicago on an extremely turbulent flight when suddenly the air masks dropped from the ceiling. Because I had flown all my life, I already knew what to do. I even reached over and helped the very well lubricated Mr. Abundance put on his mask. However, as I turned in my seat, fear seized me by the throat and I lost all use of my limbs as I heard Mary, the flying Nun, mumbling "We're going to die! We're going to die! We're going to die!" I thought to myself, *if the flying nun is losing it, I've got no hope!* It was all I could do to NOT yell, "HAIIIIIL, Mary, get a hold of yourself!" Maintaining an outwardly calm appearance, I knew that no questionable words should come out of my mouth, so instead, I calmly said, "Hail Mary full of grace, we need help right now."

Mr. Abundance handed me one of his handy little libations and suggested I pass it to the flying nun to help her feel better. It was like no Holy Communion I had ever seen, so I passed it right back to him! On this particular day, Mr. Abundance partook of the Living Vodka. Hail Mary was praying in the Spirit, and as for me ... Well, let's just say that God and I were indeed having a little chit-chat. I can safely say that we all grew in faith during this never to be forgotten flight.

On the way home from that same trip, I landed in Dallas to catch a connecting "puddle jumper" into Abilene. The problems started when we found out that the air flight controllers were on strike so the pilot would have to land the plane without instructions or extra help on this very foggy night. The only plane available would hold seven lucky people - yes, seven, that perfectly complete Biblical number. Although I probably should have stayed on the ground, I marched ahead and, against my better judgment, asked for one of the seven seats on this little Buddy Holly plane.

After a revival meeting kind of ride, we landed and slid off the runway into layers of mud and high water. As we prepared to disembark, the pilot – a frustrated comedian if there ever was one – announced, "Thank you for flying with us. We hope your flight has been all you expected and much, much more. Next time you fly, reconsider the seven seater, come-to-Jesus meeter." He then said our stewardess would help us out the door and cautioned us to watch that first step as "it's an oozy doozy!"

Another time I was flying with my mother on a jumbo jet. Bigger is better, right? However, this huge jet was jumping through the turbulence around us like a ski boat in choppy seas, jostling the passengers inside like mannequins in a crash test vehicle. In my head I could hear this little Sunday school song, "The wise man built his house upon the rock and the house on the rock stood firm." Only I was hearing this little song with a new verse, "As the plane went down, the cups went up, as the cups went down, the juice splashed out." Go ahead and sing along. This is a catchy little tune.

Fear, in fact, is the most contagious song you will ever sing. Before you know it, people around you will jump right in on the chorus and soon everyone gets swept up in the melody.

In real estate, they say it's all about location, location, location. For the comedian, it's all about timing, timing, timing. Somehow, both of these concepts eluded me so I began to overshare a bit with my mother. As the fine folks around us were now blotting the tomato juice, sodas, and smelly libations from their clothes and sifting through the rubble that had been dumped out of the emptied overhead storage bins, I announced to my mom my firm belief that when it's time to go, it's time to go. I then proceeded to overshare with the complete honesty and innocence of the young and inexperienced, telling her that when God calls you home, it is just your time. If this was the time to go, I was ready for that great celebration in the sky.

In my youthful naiveté, I had not yet realized that when my mother said, "Bless your heart," she was using her native Texan-speak to obliquely say, "You're a dingbat, but I love you anyway."

I expected in that precious moment of mother-daughter connectedness to hear her warm expression of maternal affection, but certainly anticipated nothing short of beaming pride from my doting parent as I expounded about my faith. Imagine my shock and disillusionment when she looked at me as though I had sprouted snakes out of my nostrils and firmly replied, "Well, you may be ready to go, but I am not ready to go today. I still have a lot of living to do." She then instructed the flight attendant to make sure the pilot knew he'd better land this plane safely and soon. I think she probably got a standing ovation for her stirring rendition of "Let my people LAND!"

Just Debbie...

What emotions come to your mind when you hear the words: bungee jump, free fall, and roller coaster?

Picture this: A twenty-two year old woman is poised on a lofty bridge over a raging river 365 feet below. She jumps with confidence, knowing she is securely tethered to the bridge by bungee cords. As she falls, the cords extend and stretch, but fate intervenes and the cords snap. She endures a micro-second of shock and terror as she plunges into the crocodile-infested waters below, knocking the breath from her body. The rushing river sweeps her battered and severely injured body into the rapids and on toward the falls ahead.

It sounds like a scene from an action movie or a popular video game, but it REALLY happened. The young woman found herself at home a week later with broken ribs and damaged lungs, but still very much alive ... miraculously so. The local news station asked her in an interview if she would ever consider bungee jumping again.

She answered, "I don't know."

WHAT? She doesn't know? Are you kidding me? Broken ropes, battered body, crocodile-infested waters, rapids carrying her toward the falls ... and she needs to *think* about it? My opinion is they should take some of this woman's blood and make a vaccine for the rest of us! Seriously, we should all go get our "phobia vaccination." This sounds like a promising breakthrough to me. Good-bye Xanax ... hello Bungee Booster!

The truth is, we all have our fears, but whether or not they are valid depends a lot on how old you are. If you are an adult and still afraid of Barney, the purple dinosaur who sings and dances, you might need to read another book before ours. However, there are some fears that are certainly legitimate ... snakes, heights, or anything that can take your life. I personally think crocodiles and bungee cords should be in this list, as well. We are born with this internal gauge - a life-preserving instinct - to protect ourselves from those things that can harm us.

Fear is, indeed, the most contagious song you will ever sing and it is a pretty catchy little melody. I find myself singing that same little tune over and over, except the words to the verses actually change to fit the circumstances. However, every situation fits the very same chorus, "Oh no! Oh no! I don't have a clue. I can't handle this! What will I do?" I don't know about you, but I am ready for a brand new song. I want to walk by faith ... not by fear.

The point that Denise so bravely tried to express to her mother - even though it was at the worst possible moment - is one we all have to consider at some point. It's just something we prefer to think of later ... much later. When we worry about what *might* happen, it is called fear and we focus on the *what-ifs*. If we obsess on that fear and look for ways to manipulate normal, everyday situations to avoid what scares us, that fear becomes a phobia.

When we experience a traumatic event our fear of "What if?" becomes "What's next?" In other words, we are waiting for the other shoe to drop because we have realized that shoes DO drop and that bad things don't just happen to other people. Bad things can and do happen to us. We can actually get a little stuck in the mud. Alright, some of us actually need a tow truck to pull us out and a street washer to hose us off. I understand about "being stuck in the mud" as I have a fear of flying. I will fly if I have to, but it's not my first choice.

In my life BC (before children), my husband, our associate pastor and I were all flying from Phoenix home to Tucson, Arizona. We comprised the entire church staff - senior pastor, associate pastor and worship leader - all together in one memorable plane ride. We were just a few minutes out of Tucson when I noticed the runway below was lined with emergency vehicles. There seemed to be red lights flashing as far as my eyes could see. I said to my husband, "Someone has a problem!" I personally love the fine art of denial; it is like a big fluffy pillow.

My husband replied, "We have the problem. Have you noticed we have not slowed down?" Nooooo ... I had not noticed that, and thank you so much, my dear, for ripping my comfy pillow of denial out from under me!

About this time, I began to smell something burning and our plane quickly became engulfed in thick, dark smoke. There was no time for announcements of emergency information over the PA system as the plane made a 200 mph landing with no reduction in speed. We hit the ground harder than a piano being dropped out of a 14th floor window. It was a dark, foggy night and what I remember most is the sound of babies crying.

The stewardess began yelling, "Assume crash positions! Assume crash positions!"

We not only hit the runway harder than you can possibly imagine, but the next bounce found us bumping though the grassy field that comes *after* the runway. The roar was deafening! This was life or death unfolding by the moment, and everyone knew it. I had one overwhelmingly strong thought. I knew without a doubt that in the next minute I would be alright or I would see Jesus' face. His was the only face I could see as it was happening. I just saw His smile and felt at peace.

Our associate pastor had been sitting in the back section of the plane and told us later that he had been deep in prayer since we had taken off from Phoenix. He said he had an overwhelming burden to pray for all of us. My husband and I were sitting in the first row on the right hand side of the plane. Seated beside me was a little girl who

I learned was flying back and forth between visiting her divorced parents. God had surely placed her next to me.

Our plane was filled with smoke and all the power was out. We would actually find out later that we had lost both hydraulic systems that day. The remarkably heroic pilot, with God's help, landed that plane with no hydraulics. He had to use the reverse engines to get it stopped.

You know how the flight attendants explain that the emergency chute will deploy in case of emergencies? Well, I am here to tell you that they do and it does! Another little bit of crash-landing trivia: when you exit the plane in an emergency situation, they require all of your personal items to stay on board.

So, we were preparing to exit the plane and the stewardess was trying to grab my purse to keep it on the plane. I will just tell you girls right now, that was *not* going to happen! They may have kept my hairbrush, my hairdryer, all my make-up and my entire suitcase, which might have meant that Sunday morning was going to be an entirely new au natural look for me, but they were not keeping my purse ... "No, Ma'am!"

I held tightly onto my "shield of faith", grabbed this little girl in my arms, and we were the very first two people to go down the emergency chute. Adding insult to terrified injury, as we slid down our chute, they sprayed us with emergency foam, and upon reaching the bottom, we looked up to see National Guard soldiers greeting us with rifles. It was like "Wipeout" meets "Platoon" in real life.

It was at that precise moment my soft pillow of denial vanished and my body began to shake. I quickly realized I could not feel my right arm - I have no idea how I held onto my purse and that precious little girl - and I had bruises on my arms and legs. They wanted to treat me for a neck injury at the scene; I just wanted to go home. "Shock" would be a masterpiece of understatement to describe my state at the time, but God was still at work.

Our associate pastor, with my husband's assistance, was taking pictures of everything. They talked non-stop for hours, barely pausing to take a breath. This was the single greatest adventure either of them had ever seen. Every siren-bearing vehicle in the greater Tucson area came rolling in. News reporters and cameramen were everywhere, and with so much action going on in front of their very eyes, I think they were waiting for Clint Eastwood or Arnold Schwarzenegger to roll in and check out the set. For them, it was high drama ... I was simply numb.

My husband, Ed, and I would find out the rest of the story a couple of years later. We had a pilot friend who studied our crash as part of his flight training. He told us that our plane's failure was the same hydraulic failure as the Sioux City, Iowa airline crash where most of the people died. We were seconds away from implosion. Our plane had no functioning back-up hydraulics. God, Himself, had enabled that amazing pilot to land us with barely any of the tools he needed that day.

They took pictures of us in front of the plane before we were hauled away. The fuselage of the plane had broken right where we sat in row one. Our plane was like an upside down convertible. There was no floor below our seat. Right in front of our plane was an embankment, placed there to keep airplanes from going onto the road and harming others; hitting it, however, would have caused even more damage.

The plane we were in was completely totaled in that crash landing and was retired to be studied. Yet, not one life was lost. Many gained a stronger faith that day. I know I did. I guess my oversharing friend was right. When God is with you, you can count on one of two things: He will never leave you alone in this life, or He will greet you with a smile in the next. Either way, it's all good. It is impossible for the enemy to defeat a Spirit-filled Christian. You can't take us ANYWHERE until GOD calls us HOME.

A few years after our crash landing, Ed and I felt God calling us to leave a ministry situation that was not glorifying Him. My husband prayed about this and felt we needed to take a stand by resigning, yet we had no place to go. The very day we resigned from that ministry, we came home wondering what we would do and where we would go.

We opened the mailbox and there was a large settlement check from the airlines for my injuries.

I will never choose to bungee jump, free fall, or ride any more "loop- de- loop" rides. I had my fill of thrill rides that life-changing day. If you are reading this chapter and you find yourself afraid of anything – free falls, heights, depths, the future, the powers that govern our world, or even demons – I want you to know that I totally "get" where you are coming from. However, GET THIS and get it good: GOD IS GOOD and He is always working GOOD. No matter what it involves, no matter how long, high, wide, or big your free fall may seem to you ... God is still sovereign.

The enemy may do his very best to attack us, and he may do his best to wear us down. However, we all need to remember an important lesson from Job. God allows the enemy to tempt us in this fallen world, but make no mistake about it, our God is still GOD. The book of Job is in the Bible to prepare us for the trials that will come our way. In it, I find some important things that we need to remember when we find ourselves free falling.

In the first chapter of Job we see that Satan comes with the angels to talk to God, who is speaking very highly of his servant Job. God is very proud of Job, a righteous man.

Job 1:1b (NIV) tells us, "This man was blameless and upright; he feared God and shunned evil." Satan can't stand this. He truly believes that all humans should have to pay a price for their loyalty to God. So he replies to God, "Does Job fear God for nothing? Have you not put a hedge around him and his household and everything he has?" (Job 1:9a NIV). Satan goes on to ask God to stretch out His hand and strike everything that Job has because he believes that Job will then curse God. God gives Satan permission to attack Job, but tells him not to lay a finger on Job's physical being.

Satan attacks Job and takes away everything he has, but he still can't get Job to sin against God in any way. This is one faithful man! So Satan comes back into God's presence and says, "Skin for skin...a man will give all he has for his own life" (Job 2:4 NIV). Satan then asks

God for permission to actually harm Job, himself, as he has already attacked his family and all he owns. God tells Satan that he must spare Job's life. Job 2:7b (NIV) then tells us that Job is afflicted with "painful sores from the soles of his feet to the top of his head."

Job is being accused throughout the entire book by his so-called friends. They are all trying to analyze him and point out his sin. Meanwhile, back at the ranch ... or lack of it ... Job's wife is telling him to curse God and die. She, obviously, is not the encourager in the family or the one that God was bragging about as being righteous and blameless.

How does Job react to such devastation, personal attacks, pain and suffering? Job 3:24b-26 (NIV) tells us his response, "My groans pour out like water ... what I feared has come upon me; what I dreaded has happened to me. I have no peace, no quietness; I have no rest, but only turmoil."

This man is in extreme free fall mode. He is spiraling down, down, down ...

Somehow I can picture Johnny Cash there, all dressed in black, just singing away, "Down, down, down, and the flames went higher." Job's life was worse than any country western song you have ever heard. He lost everything but "the girl", and she continued to heap it on his poor, bowed head. If he had been a less righteous man, he probably would have wished his boils on her, or worse! What was Job supposed to do while he was facing extreme suffering and what was he NOT supposed to do?

Job 1:22 (NIV) sheds light on an important principle for all of us to hang onto in troubled times. It simply says: "In ALL THIS Job did NOT sin by charging God with wrongdoing." (Emphasis added.) Sin is when we rebel, make ourselves the judge, and question God, attributing wrong to him.

The end of the story describes God talking to Job. We all would do well to read this passage each and every day. Let me just leave you with one question that God asks Job.

"Does the eagle soar at your command and build its nest on high?" (Job 39:27 NIV).

When we are free falling, do we understand that it is God, alone, who causes the eagle and the hawk to soar? They fly through His mighty power alone.

Job's response shows a new understanding of everything God has told him. In Job 42:2 (NIV) he says, "I know that you can do all things; **no purpose** of yours can be thwarted." (Emphasis added.) Did you catch the part about none of God's plans can be thwarted? The phrase there was "**NO Purpose**". That means none ... Nada ... **N-O -- W-A-Y!**

Have you ever feared that the enemy has won? He has **NOT**.

Ever felt like God needs you to tell Him how to run *His* business? He does **NOT**.

Have you ever thought that life is unfair and that it is all about you? It is **NOT**.

Not only did God deal with Job, but He also dealt with Job's so-called friends. This happened differently than you might ever dream. The Bible said, "After Job prayed for his friends the Lord restored his fortunes and gave him twice as much as he had before" (Job 42:10 NIV). These men had spent the entire time trying to point out Job's supposed wrongs and had accused him daily.

The book of Job ends like this, "The Lord blessed the latter part of Job's life more than the first" (Job 42:12a NIV). So, not only are we never to blame God, but we are not to blame others who wrong us. It was when Job forgave his so-called friends that he was completely restored. The end of his life was even stronger than his blessed beginning.

It is common to start believing that those who are going through hard times must be in some kind of sin. The book of Job tells us otherwise. Job's friends were not the only ones guilty of finger-pointing in times of suffering. When trials, loss, and suffering come, we can rest assured that the enemy wants us to curse God. Satan pours on the pressure so we will accuse God of wrong doing. He wants to separate us from God. That's his goal: to get us down, defeat us, and cause us to lose faith in our all-powerful God.

You can fly or drive. You can cruise or snooze. You can take a train, a bus, or a little yellow taxi. You may sign up to parasail, free fall, or bungee jump, or you can just sit at home in your big ol' easy chair. The truth is that trouble can find you in any of those places. Yet, we are always safe in the arms of God, and His arms can reach anywhere.

If you ever find yourself in that awful, fearful, free fall, sing out, "Blessed be the name of the Lord, Blessed be His glorious name!" Sing it loud, and sing it with all your might! God always responds to the praises of His people.

The next time you find yourself free-falling make sure you know who holds the other end of your bungee cord ... and remember who lovingly holds your hand.

Tubular Therapy Thought

Like Job, we will be tested, and will find that our family and friends will fail us. Job did not blame God for his troubles and when he forgave, he was blessed and restored. The end of his life was even better than his beginning. A blessed life is a life that exemplifies forgiveness.

CHAPTER SIX

It All Depends

(This is funny Denise guarding the door of the "facilities" while flying…from now on when you fly you will be reminded of Denise's Depend wearing grandma, a marine, and an "Oo-Rah"!)

"Above all, love each other deeply,
because love covers a multitude of sins."
(I Peter 4:8 NIV)

Funny Denise ...

Isn't it funny how you come into this world wearing diapers ... and you leave this world wearing depends? Your mother tries desperately to get you out of the diapers, and your children try desperately to get you back into them.

I have issues. I have had these issues with sneezing, coughing, laughing and the like for years, but the minute I turned 40 they became known as, "The time of my life with my BFF, Mr. Depend." I'd like to say it rarely happens to me, but that would be a very loose interpretation of truth.

I had the joy and pleasure to have my grandmother in my life for a short period of time as an adult and it provided some of my fondest memories. She taught me all about the Depend. But the funniest memory of my grandmother was the plane ride from Indiana back to California.

Mom and I had flown from San Diego to Ft. Wayne, Indiana to pick up my grandmother who was coming to stay with my parents. We boarded a flight and found our seats about 7 rows from the back of the plane with Mom in the window seat, Grandma in the middle and me on the aisle. As Mom slept, Grandma leaned over to me and said "Denny, I need to go to the facilities." I got us both unbuckled and out to the main aisle to discover, of course, a line.

Finally, we got to the restroom and she said, "Come in here and help me, please." I thought to myself, *it's a CLOSET and not even a walk-in closet!* I said, "Grandma, darlin', you and I both can't get in that bathroom and close the door."

She said, "Well I can't do this alone."

I thought, *you can't do WHAT alone?* But I said, "Ok, Hun. We'll try."

Now something you don't know about me is that I come from a long line of chunky derrieres. We may be tall, but you could set a three-course place setting on our backsides. So, Grandma and I pushed and squeezed until we were both inside that bathroom. I tried to shut the door, but had run out of room ... her derriere, my derriere ... you get the picture! Trust me - the full story would be an overshare.

Luckily, right behind me was a Marine, dressed to impress. He said, "Ma'am, I would be honored to stand guard for you in front of this door so you can help your grandmother." They say a Marine "never leaves a man behind" and we certainly needed help with her behind on this particular day, so I just said, "Oo-Rah!" He and I were now a team on a top-secret, covert, highly classified mission! This was "Mission Impossible!" He was covering the front, and I had the rear.

He turned away, arms across his chest. I couldn't see daylight if I tried. I looked at Grandma and said, "Ok, Sweets ... let's get this mission started!" She then began a process that, to this day, I laugh about every time I go to the bathroom.

She lifted her shirt and said, "That's one." She pulled down her pants and said, "That's two." She pulled down her panty hose and said, "That's three." She pulled down her granny panties and said, "That's four." She pulled down her full set of Depends and said, "That's five." She then squatted down and smiled at me!

I said, "Grandma, what's with the counting?"

She just kept mouthing the word "five" to me over and over again. When she was finished, she stood up and began to put everything back on, counting the various stages of dress in reverse back to one.

I asked, again, as she was washing her hands what that counting was all about. She said, "At my age, I need to count how many layers I have on and make sure that what comes down lifts right back up.

Once I was in a dress and didn't count the layers and couldn't figure out why I couldn't walk very well. I couldn't get my legs apart very far. That night I realized I forgot to pull up my Depend."

I looked over my shoulder at the Marine and his shoulders were shaking from laughter. I know he was thinking, "Oo- Rah!" because, frankly, I was too.

Now many in my family will tell you that I got my wild sense of humor from my Depend-wearing grandma, but I also inherited from her some other not-so-lovely traits.

It was a beautiful fall Saturday morning. I was in charge of leading a group of women from our church up to Julian in the mountains for a one day women's retreat. I jumped in my little sports car and began to lead a parade of about seven cars through the desert and up the mountains to a gorgeous cabin for a relaxing day of laughter and food.

We started our trek through the desert and turned past the checkpoint to go up the mountain. I wasn't exactly sure how much further we had to drive, but it was a lovely day so it really didn't matter, until my bladder decided otherwise, and the pressure mounted.

Suddenly, my brain was having an argument with my bladder that went something like this ...

Bladder: "I need the facilities, NOW!"

Brain: "It's not much further...you can hold it."

Bladder: "WRONG!! I'm about to explode!"

Brain: "Think positive! You can DO THIS!"

Bladder: "I'm not designed to THINK!"

Brain: "OK, OK! Don't get your panties in a knot. We will pull over ..."

I pulled over to the side of the road and so did the other seven cars behind me. How in the world would I explain to these ladies that I had to visit the little girl's room when there was no restroom in sight? I got out of the car and explained quickly that I just couldn't hold it any longer and needed to find a place to "count the layers."

To one side of me was a mountain ... straight up. To the other side of me was a cliff ... straight down. Since that seemed to be the best option for privacy, I chose to climb down the cliff, thinking to myself, *It's not that far. There are branches to grab and you need to be far enough over the side so no one can see you. You can do this. It's not rocket science.*

I began the slow process of climbing down the cliff, but my first step started an avalanche of sand and dirt and I slid derriere first, hitting every brush and rock for 20 feet until I reached the next outcropping of rock.

Whew, I thought, *at least I stopped and am miraculously still dry!* I found a convenient bush for privacy and began "counting my layers." As I "hovered," I admired the majestic vista from my private little ledge. Before me stretched a beautiful desert valley surrounded by towering mountains with the most beautiful trees, and I could even see some bright orange flowers in the distance.

While I admired the lovely scenery, I noticed the orange flowers seemed to be moving. Were my eyes playing tricks on me, or what? Then I heard a sound that no one with their granny panties down around their ankles ever wants to hear ... gunshots! Yep ... there I was in all my glory watching God's scenery. Apparently about 20 hunters – with binoculars - were also admiring the view, watching MY scenery!

I hastily dragged on my clothes, made a grab for my dignity, and made a running start to climb back up the cliff. With each step, I slid right back down to the bottom of the cliff. I tried grabbing hold of the brush to heave myself up, but the roots were so shallow they just pulled right out of the ground, and back down I would slide.

Several rapid-fire thoughts crossed my mind almost simultaneously:

How long would I have to stay down there before someone would realize I was missing?

Would they send the Cavalry? Better yet, where was that nice Marine? I certainly needed someone to not leave anything behind right now!

How many hunter magazine covers would display my bare derriere squatted over a bush? Could I sue for invasion of privacy or would I be sued for public display of my "assets"?

Did I know any of those hunters and would I have to face them on Monday morning at work ... or worse, Sunday morning at church?

The questions went on and on for what seemed like an eternity.

After 15 minutes of trying over and over to climb the cliff, I was within one giant step of reaching the top when I realized I was slipping again and made one last-ditch effort.

I put one leg up as far as I could reach and bounced on the other leg two or three times before catapulting myself into the air. The momentum of the counterweight provided by my family legacy had a lot to do with getting me over the edge. All I can tell you is that I remember seeing my life flash before my eyes and then I came to rest knees first on the nearest slab of highway.

I had thought somebody would come to my rescue in the midst of my predicament, but no one did. I imagined my grandma's view of my plight from Heaven, and knew she understood. I found myself wishing I had a guardian angel like Grandma's Marine from the airplane. Nevertheless, I made it back alive, so I just had to say, "Oo-Rah!"

My little group of ladies just stared and pointed at me as they made a lame attempt to cover their laughter. I got up, brushed myself off, gathered my tattered pride and walked slowly back to my vehicle. I climbed in the car, put it in Drive and continued up the mountain. I remember thinking to myself *I wish my best friend would have been here.*

One thing I learned on both occasions is that we all need someone to cover our back sometime. That scenic day in the mountain with the little down-hill slide, hunters in orange, and the lovely face plant on the highway, well, that was my sometime!

So, girlfriend, if you are reading this book and you have recently encountered a down- hill slide of embarrassing proportions, I feel your pain. We are here with you to cover your back-side and throw in a little "Oo-Rah!" as needed.

Just Debbie...

The truth of the matter is simply this: There is a thin line between hilarity and humiliation. Perhaps the difference is whether or not we know our real worth when it all goes south? We have all had those awful moments in life when we are simply out for a joy ride on a beautiful autumn day and along comes the unexpected. Suddenly, our humanity takes us on an unplanned side trip, and before we know it, we are grabbing at everything around us, trying to hold on for dear life.

Have you ever felt at those unexpected moments like a bunch of hunters have their binoculars pointed straight at you? As the shame begins to roll over you, your next thought is, *I am alone; I am going down, and I desperately need a hand to lift me up.* As you emerge from the rubble, you begin looking at the sea of faces around you. Perhaps, like me, you know them all from church. They are the Bible study girls, the choir sisters, or the deaconess darlings. But the real question is: "Can I depend on someone?"

The irony of that day is Denise was headed to a women's day of fellowship, but the real fellowship she needed was a "hand up" before she even got there. We often think that life is about the destination, but the truth is, it is really more about the journey.

Do we sit in church or choose to be THE CHURCH? Do we sit in our pew week after week, waiting for someone to reach out to us, or do we remember how it feels to need that helping hand and reach out to others? Will we take the time to make those connections that will provide us with a lifeline in our day of trouble, or will we sit in solitude and fall in adversity, unable to get ourselves back up?

A few years before Denise's autumn drive and subsequent face plant on the mountain, I faced a season in my life that was much like the day she just described. I felt alone and so in need of a hand up, and I prayed that God would send me a friend. I was serving in a church that was beautiful on the outside, but sorely lacking of godly graces on the inside.

Like Denise's "mountain slide experience" I was also in need of the fellowship that comes from a church that offers a hand-up.

Take it from Denise's little Depend-wearing, layer-counting grandma: we were never intended to face life's challenges alone. We all need a friend to walk with, laugh with, and count the layers with us. You know, come to think of it, God is a lot like that big strong Marine with his arms crossed, guarding the door who said, "Ma'am, it would be my honor to protect and watch over you."

Now **THAT** is something to "Oo-Rah" about!

Tubular Therapy Thought

The Bible reminds us that we all will fall down and need a hand up. Not only that but we may seriously be in trouble if we are left to ourselves.

A true friend always covers your back...*"Oo-Rah"!*

CHAPTER SEVEN
Hot Stone Massage

(Just so you know, these brown washcloths at Walmart are much larger than the little-itsy-bitsy ones at the Vichy shower!)

"No discipline seems pleasant at the time, but painful. Later on, however, it produces a harvest of righteousness and peace for those who have been trained by it. Therefore, strengthen your feeble arms and weak knees."
(Heb. 12:11-12 NIV)

Funny Denise...

A popular treatment these days is called the Hot Stone Massage. I, however, do not like heat, pressure, or pain. So, the very thought of a massage or of hot rocks being applied to my body has never, EVER called my name. Well, not until recently ...

Ever have a friend who comes up with bright ideas that absolutely scare you to death every time you are together? For years, Debbie's plans have always been to get me in the water – a pool, a lazy river, a lake, or an ocean. All of these frighten me beyond words, but nothing has scared me as much as the day Debbie decided I needed to go for a massage. My neck was tight and my back was hurting from work and she decided it would be just the thing to make me feel better. That was the day I learned there was something I feared even more than water.

"The massage," she said, "will help rid your body of toxins."

Now doesn't that just sound peachy?

As she described how wonderful a massage would be, how great I would feel afterwards, and that I didn't have to be TOTALLY NAKED.

Wait! ... Did she just say naked?

I pleaded with her to take me to a lake; at least there I could wear a swimsuit. I felt desperate. She laughed and told me this would be a wonderful experience. What was running through my mind was how I would have to apologize to the masseuse each time she touched my back fat and it rolled into a ball. The very thought of having someone massage my naked abundance made me nervously conjure up all of the embarrassing bodily functions that could possibly happen. At your first appointment they have you fill out a form detailing what body parts you want massaged. I guess I should have paid more attention to anatomy when I was in high school because I thought if you were going to get a massage, you better get your money's worth. I also wished someone would have told me what "glutes" meant.

My first masseuse, let's just call her Greta, was six foot two and she could probably bench press a small vehicle. When she called my name the hairs stood up on the back of my neck. Greta took me into this room and told me to strip down until I was comfortable, so I took my shoes off. She said to get under the sheets on the bed face down.

Now for those of you who don't know, there is a place to put your face. I call it "de hole". So when Greta came back in, she told me to put my face in "de hole". I said, "It's OK, I will lay with my head sideways." Greta then threw a towel over my face and I couldn't breathe, so I took it off. She put it back on and I slipped it off; it was a "Swedish Stand-off."

She began to massage my back and it actually felt pretty good so I began to relax. My knotted muscles began to unwind, and other body parts began to loosen up, also. The elevator music was making soothing little "chink-a-chink" sounds and within minutes I was SNORING. Our symphony sounded something like this: "Chink-a-Chink, ZZZZZZZZZ," and then, "PUFFFFFFFT!"

I was suddenly awake, embarrassed and a little frightened. I might have gotten away with this little involuntary release if Greta had not decided at exactly that moment to lift the sheets and ask me to roll over.

I knew Greta had gotten a whiff when she stopped mid-sentence. Who is a woman to blame in this situation? After all there were only two of us in that little room, and there was no dog in sight. So, I looked at Greta and said, "That was some bad lotion. Do you use skunk oil here?"

Greased-lightning Greta quickly stepped away from the table and busied herself momentarily in a new location. Now I refer to her as "Greta the Glute Meister" because, although I was not at all fond of anyone touching me any place near my glutes, she proceeded to tell me how tight my lower back was. Before I knew it, Greta was bearing down on me with the full force of her Volkswagen-lifting arms. I suddenly felt an inexpressible need to apologize for my glutes not being in the general vicinity of where they had started out.

After the Glute Meister experience, Debbie and I came up with a few handy rules before our next little outing:

Rule #1: Use the restroom before you lie down.

Rule #2: Keep in mind all the words you learned in anatomy class. The word "Glute" should always be followed by the words, "No thank-you".

Rule #3: It is really best to try to stay awake during a massage. This will prevent noises, and the blaming that may follow additional sounds beside the chink-a-chink music.

Rule #4: Always be brutally honest.

We have learned our lessons through compiling our experiences and feel obligated to pass these rules on to all our friends. You can take it as wise advice or fair warning ... your choice.

One time, Debbie and I convinced our pregnant friend to get a massage. We told her all of the marvelous benefits and Debbie gave her the "Toxin Be Gone" speech, telling her how great she would feel. I am really not sure if Debbie covered the "partially naked" information or not. In hindsight, perhaps we overlooked a few things. Anyway, we forgot to tell her Rule # 4: Always be brutally honest.

This sweet girl went in for her first massage and looked up to see her masseuse pulling out a pair of latex gloves which she firmly pulled on and snapped at her wrists saying, "Would it be OK if I do your massage today with latex gloves on?"

Now, I don't know how that hits you, but for me that is just way too much like going in for that certain annual exam that everyone dreads. Our friend's first thought was, *if she brings out any lubricant, I'm out of here!* Seriously wondering if she had taken a wrong turn walking down the hallway, she thought she might have gone into a doctor's office by mistake. She was caught completely off-guard and left speechless.

Her masseuse went on to say that she had a rash all over her arms and did not have a doctor's appointment until tomorrow, thus the latex gloves. She didn't think she was contagious, but she really didn't know yet. This, my dear friends, is why we came up with Rule #4. Write this rule down and memorize it. You may never know when it will come in handy. Our poor friend had her first massage at the hands of "Latex Lucy."

Sometimes we just need to practice the word NO and stick with it. Some of you dear ladies may think we are making this up, but I assure you we are not. You can ask our sweet, dear friend, Becca, because she will never forget that outing nor will she go on any future massage outings with the likes of us! I don't blame her at all as I know just how she feels.

The new rage in massages these days is the Hot Stone Massage. The whole premise behind this is that the hot stones will help relax all the tension in the muscles. At the very least, you will look like you got a suntan, and at worst you may feel like a loaf of bread in an oven. If you are lucky enough to have someone like Greta, you'll also get your buns kneaded; this is why I have SO FAR abstained from this kind of massage. In fact, I think I may have invented a brand new phobia. I call it "Gret-a-phobia" as just the thought of that Glute Meister with hot stones in her hands has me scared silly ... very silly!

I must admit, however, that I have learned so much since my first massage. I don't know if those harmful toxins ever really left my body, but I certainly have felt the weight of the world drop away through the resulting laughter.

Just Debbie...

The Bible tells us the story of David and Bathsheba. The trouble began because Bathsheba was taking a roof top bath and David saw it. Nothing good ever comes from a rooftop bath. I have read the Bible and as a preacher's kid, I should know this story. However, I had to experience some things up-close before I made the connection.

My husband (the man of the cloth) and I decided to get a couple's rooftop massage in sunny Tucson, Arizona during our stay at a lovely resort there. This sounded like a wonderfully romantic idea to both of us.

For anyone who does not know, Tucson is in the desert, and summer temperatures get really, really hot! Truthfully, I wasn't feeling well before we went up there, but when we stood up to leave in our matching fluffy white robes, I saw big, black, **hot massage stones** swimming before my eyes, and that was all she wrote. I apparently blacked out and an ambulance came and took me away. The good news is that when I awoke, the nice resort had said I could keep my fluffy white robe as I had nothing on underneath. What a bargain! I got a free ride, a new robe, and another rule for my list: When you are on a rooftop, remember the Old Testament story and keep your clothes on. It will turn out better for everyone.

I am sure that by now you are thinking I would have learned from my mistakes, and you may be wondering why I would take others to massage centers for this unusual punishment. Misery loves company, I guess. I evidently still have a lot to learn.

My husband is an excellent golfer and frequently wins golf tournaments. That means he often gets to bring home a prize. When that happens, he is so pleased with himself because he can give me lovely gifts without his wallet feeling a twinge. One year I got a free pair of Ugg boots which are so sparkly, cute, and toasty warm. I just love them!

After another golf tournament, he gave me a certificate for a massage and a "Vichy" shower. *How lovely! I thought to myself.* Perhaps you too are wondering, *what in the world is a "Vichy" shower?* I had never heard of such a thing, but I am adventurous and couldn't wait to make my appointment.

Perhaps I should have done my research first, as I found out later that the word "Vichy" means NAKED. If I had only known that one little word, it would have altered my entire day. However, there is nothing like the element of surprise.

The "Vichy" shower looks like a big MRI spa machine, only your head sticks out so you can yell when the going gets tough or when the (not so) tough really needs to get going.

A nice lady came in and told me to get undressed and sit on the ledge of the Aqua machine. Then she handed me two of the smallest washcloths I had ever seen, and told me that I could cover up my special parts with these.

Really? Seriously? I thought to myself ... That is going to do it? I wondered which two of my three special parts I should cover because these wash cloths were smaller than a bikini and not nearly as cute. I asked for a third.

She opened the lid on this thing that looked like a mummy's chamber with running water. *I was going to be embalmed?!?*

As I was thinking, "*... to my son I leave my car, my good looks and my musical talents ... and to my daughter I leave all the movies, snacks, my sense of humor and party planning antics ...*" my thoughts were rudely interrupted by the Vichy Embalmer opening the tomb and saying, "In you go!"

I lie down flat covered by two (OK, three) tiny brown fig leaves with no cell phone which I had no place to put anyway.

Trying to come up with an intelligent question I asked, "How do people usually like this treatment?"

This **DIVA** (**D**eadly **I**nternment **V**ichy **A**ttendant) said, "Well, people either love it or they hate it. I'll be back in a little while. Just call if you need anything."

At first I was just lying there, but that was not working out too well for me. Soon I began to feel the first hint of anxiety, similar to what you feel after the elevator doors have closed and don't open again, so I began praying. Shortly after that I tried singing, then "praying in the spirit", but none of these diversions was really helping. The water was continuing to get hotter; I was rapidly heating up, inside and out. Do you know that stage of life where anything that upsets you can cause a chain reaction, and you soon start to feel like you are about to spontaneously combust? I refer to it as a *power surge*. That day, my *surge* could have run a nuclear power plant.

I was stuck, locked in this Vichy Aqua Torture Chamber and there was no escape. What kind of ding-ding would put the release handle on the outside? I'm not judging ... I'm just sayin' ...! You are probably wondering where a woman wearing three small brown wash cloths can go in a situation like this. I was wondering the same thing. I had only been in the mummy's chamber for about ten minutes; I was "laid bare before the throne of God" and it was about time for the invitation hymn. I was thinking of the old hymn that I grew up singing each and every Sunday, "Just as I am". Yes, that song just about summed it up.

I decided it was time for a jail break. I needed out, and I needed out <u>NOW</u>! No one was in the room with me, so, with no thought for the ladies in the waiting room or those who were trying to enjoy themselves and relax while getting their hair and nails done, I began the call of the wild that would have made Tarzan proud! My middle name isn't Jane for nothing! I sounded like a caged animal, or worse, like any imprisoned, almost naked, menopausal woman in need of freedom and cool air.

"Hello!! Is anyone out there? Helloooo, I'm in here!" Like a symphony building to that final crescendo, my melodic voice was rising ... Rising ... RISING ... "GET ME OUT OF HERE!!!!!!!!!!" The lady rolled back the stone and out of the tomb I arose, three washcloths to the wind!

There were so many lovely ladies in the waiting room that fine day. I can only hope I didn't traumatize any of them too badly. And, the lady that was working at the desk was, of course, related to a lady in our church. Oh well, what's a girl to do?

All I can say about this particular massage outing is that I am a little nervous about my husband's next golf tournament prize. What if the Colonic Hydrotherapy people are running a promotional campaign? Now that's a special kind of aqua therapy I think I'll forego. I shudder at the thought, and claim God's promise that, "Each day has enough trouble of its own. Why borrow tomorrow's worries?"

I must admit that I am a dreamer and that can come with its own set of problems. I dream of things that never were and say "Why not?" Shouldn't life be like the perfect massage commercial? I envision myself on a long white sandy beach in a beautiful Jacuzzi bath, the candles are lit and all of life's problems are long forgotten. Who would ever dream there could be pain associated with making those big knots in my back just melt away?

Not only is our body filled with toxins, but so is our soul. The Bible calls it sin. This little word is no more popular today than the word toxins, but we all know that our hearts are filled to the brim with selfishness, jealousy, anger, rage, pride, bitterness, and unforgiveness.

God, himself, meets us in our little room and asks, "What part hurts? Where do you need me to begin working?" We say, "Oh no, God, not there. Don't look there. I can figure this out myself. I just want this whole experience to feel good. I don't want any pain."

Sometimes God even applies a little pressure, when necessary because He sees the hurt in places we would never recognize. The book of Revelation tells us that God wants us to be hot or cold. He will never settle for lukewarm, and so He applies the hot stones of His Word to the knots in our lives. He is the master masseuse. He rebukes, corrects, and trains us for righteousness.

Do you know that God only corrects those He loves? He corrects His children, those that belong to Him. He is not kneading your sore spots to hurt you. He is attempting to bring hope and healing to your life. The next time you are feeling a little sore, toxic, and down, remember our last and final rule: *Pick the right Masseuse!*

Just skip: "Greta the Glute Meister", "Latex Lucy", and *please* don't even consider the Vichy shower! If you decide to try the rooftop massage, be careful ... very, very careful!

Here is what I have discovered about the fine art of massage. We all want "the toxins to be gone", but we don't want the HOT STONES associated with massage. We want life to be comfy, cozy, and to keep the fluffy white robes. When the temperatures rise, God is refining us to burn away the chaff so that He can purify us. God disciplines those He loves and He always responds to those who are in need of His healing touch. His hot stones will warm your soul through and through. Sometimes we just need to pray.

"Good morning, God! This is me again. My mind, my heart, and my body really hurt today. I am in need of your healing touch; create in me a clean heart and restore my joy to me this day. Oh, and let those ugly 'toxins' be gone as I forgive the 'Latex Lucy's' in my life. I place my life in your loving hands. Amen."

Tubular  Therapy Thought

Pick the right Masseuse; and remember that God disciplines those He loves. His hot stones will warm your soul and heal your heart.

CHAPTER EIGHT

A Bad Hair Day

*(Visiting Irsula, our friend and hairdresser, and praying
for a miracle in the "bangs department"!)*

*"And over all these virtues put on love,
which binds them all together in perfect unity."*
(Colossians 3:14 NIV)

Funny Denise...

As women, there is nothing more important to us than our hair, our long, flowing, gorgeous hair. It is our crown of glory, our essence of youth, and our constant struggle. Nothing can ruin a good day like bad hair!

It was a Saturday and mom was going shopping. Even at my young age I understood the concept of retail therapy. I wanted new clothes for school and this was my chance! I got up and took a shower, got dressed, ate my breakfast and was ready to walk out the door when she looked at me and said, "No I don't think you are going today. Your hair is a mess and I am embarrassed."

Wow! My hair may have resembled a squirrel who had gathered enough nuts for the winter and tucked them beneath its golden locks, but that wasn't any reason for her to dismiss me from retail therapy, was it? I had to think fast!

I looked at her with a solemn face and said, "Mom, I will get it cut. Just say when and where, and I am there!"

She gathered her things and off we went to the beauty shop. Now, Dorothy Hamill was an icon in those days, and to have her cute pixie haircut was every young girl's dream, including mine. Mom knew she had one shot at this haircut and it had to be short and quick as my dad would never allow such a travesty in his household. We got to the beauty shop and she told the beautician to give me a "Hamill." I could see the beautician shaking her head no, but my mom was emphatic. Thirty minutes later I stared at the floor as they were sweeping away years of growth. My curly locks were piled everywhere! When they turned me around to see my new *"DO"*, I thought I was staring right at Dorothy Hamill, herself!

What I didn't realize was how much time the beautician had taken to fix my hair, pulling and straightening it so it would look right, cut that way. The next day was Sunday, so I didn't mess with perfection before hurrying off to church. However, Monday morning was picture day at school and I had to look just perfect, so I took my shower and started to do my hair. Now you need to understand that long hair is heavy and pulls the curls down. Short hair, on the other hand, does just the opposite. My hair was a curly mess and oh so much shorter without the pull of gravity to prevent shrinkage! Mom tried to work with it, but there was no hope that morning.

She finally just smiled at me and said, "It'll be ok; just smile and the picture will be wonderful."

On the way to school that morning it began to drizzle, and I swear my hair shrunk even more! By the time I got to school, I looked like Shirley Temple on a bad hair day. My ears were sticking out and curls were everywhere … and not pretty little ringlets, like you might imagine. My hair was upset and obviously rebelling! No doubt about it – it was doing its own thing and there was no stopping or controlling it. I had hair sticking out the left side of my head, and hair curled straight up on top. It was a mess. A royal mess! The photographer had a lady there to fix your hair before each shot if you needed help. She walked toward me with a comb, stopped short, shook her head and said, "Honey child, I have no WAY of helping you out! Just smile pretty and pray hard!"

I remember what I looked like that day, not because my mom put those pictures up in a frame like all the rest, and not because she sent them out to all our relatives. Oh no! I remember what I looked like on that disastrous day because, to this day, she has them in the original packet they came in, neatly tucked inside her desk drawer NEVER to be seen by the outside world! Not only do I remember the pictures that still reside in the desk drawer, but I will always remember the look on my mother's face and her famous last words, "Don't worry. We can fix this."

What I did not know at the time was that my sweet mother had modeled for me how to give compassion to someone who had been affected by "shear" terror. In the ensuing years, whenever the situation called for it, I would hear my sweet mother's voice coming out of my own mouth, "Don't worry, we can fix this."

It seems generational lies are passed down just to keep our fragile female egos intact. In the years to come, I would remember everything she modeled for me. If we are truthful, we all need a little help sometimes.

Debbie introduced me to you by telling you that we are a lot like Lucy and Ethel from "I Love Lucy." In fact, many kind, well-meaning souls have told us that. I will also admit that I look more like Lucy; my personality is similar to Lucy's, and I also collect Lucy memorabilia. However, Debbie is the one who has Lucy's spirit. If there are grapes to be stomped, she will find them. If there is medicine to take, she will find a way to skip it. If there is candy to inspect, she will hide it in her hat because she cannot possibly begin to count it. In summary, she has a way of getting herself into Lucy-esque situations, and you know Lucy never did anything without Ethel.

Her life is like one big TV series; the girl remains pretty much the same, but it is the episodes that change. We will call this episode "The Three Stooges" with Debbie playing the role of "Moe". In fact, our entire church will never forget this episode as it went "Sunday Morning Live" with a skit about her bangs.

I was having a rough day at work so I called Debbie and asked where she was so I could bring her lunch. She said she would be at church in a few minutes and to meet her by her office. I was standing on the steps outside her office with lunch in hand when she showed up. She looked disheveled and I chalked it up to the fact that she had probably been swimming and just neglected to do anything with her hair. The longer I stood there the quieter she was and the more I found myself staring at her hair.

Finally I broke the silence and said, "Did you just crawl out of bed or what?"

She said, "Can't you tell what happened?"

I said, "You lost your comb? You forgot how to comb your hair? You got bad shampoo? ... Any of these scenarios working for you?"

She said, "I went to get my bangs trimmed. I asked for 'wispies' and THIS is what I got. There are entire chunks missing from my hair!"

I said, "Oh my goodness, your bangs are *so* short! Actually, they are non-existent. Where did they go?" She just stared at me as I continued my rampage of questions, "Where did you go? Did you pay her? Did you go to the beauty school and get the girl at the bottom of the class?"

She said, "I went to the mall. I paid her. I think she just got out of beauty school and she must have failed!"

We went inside to view the damage in the light and it was worse than I could have imagined.

I said, "Where is a brush? I can fix this ..." Typical answer for all BFFs in crisis mode! She handed me her brush and actually looked at me with a glimmer of hope that I could fix this situation. On my best day I can manage a brush, but I am no magic genie!

I began to brush back the stubble so it would stand up and look fuller. It stood up alright but there was nothing full about it. I decided to gather from the back and comb forward, but the hair stopped about ¼ of an inch short of her hairline. She had 'wispies' alright but they weren't what she had imagined or asked for. She had one strand of hair about two inches long, the next strand ⅛ of an inch long, and so forth. It looked like a two year old had cut her hair while she slept.

Even I will admit my next question was ill-advised.

"Did you fall asleep during this and wake up to see this issue, or did you actually sit there, being the polite PK, and let her destroy your hair without saying a word?"

Debbie politely told me she was wide awake, but not facing the mirror and this is what she saw when she was turned around to view the product of the scissor fiasco.

"Did you fix it?" she asked.

"Just about ..." I replied, but who was I kidding? It was a nightmare and there wasn't enough hair to fix ANYTHING! About that time another one of our friends came strolling into her office and she actually GASPED when she saw Debbie.

She tried to fix the wispies, too, but to no avail. I said, "Did you show the preacher?"

"No, I didn't ..." she whispered.

I volunteered, "Well ... let's get this over with while you have friends around to cheer you up."

So off we went to the church office. You would think a "Man of God" would speak kindly to his bride, but as her husband, "the Preacher" came out of his office, his eyes became the size of 50 cent pieces and he said, "Maybe you can get fake bangs."

Believe me! That was the mistake of a lifetime and it has been memorialized in our church pictorial directory for years to come. Debbie decided to get fake bangs and have them trimmed and colored to match her hair. I would like to tell you that her new fake hair wasn't that noticeable, but I would be lying through my teeth!

Debbie sent me a text message that evening before Soup and Salad at the church and asked me to meet her outside. I knew it must be bad for her to not want to get out of the car. I braced myself because I didn't want my reaction to add to her panic. I walked outside and decided I should have taken a few more minutes to prepare myself. It was AWFUL! With her new bangs, she looked like Moe from the Three Stooges!

"Dude," I said. "You need to poof those puppies up and comb them to match."

"I did," she replied. "This is the best they are going to be. Can you tell they are fake?"

I considered my options. The cold hard truth would just be cruel. The "I don't want to hurt your feelings" answer had some appeal, but given her precarious emotional state, I decided against it. I decided a quick prayer never hurt, so I went with the "Oh dear Lord, don't let me open my mouth and insert my foot" answer.

Why is it that a good haircut needs to be cut again in two weeks but a bad haircut takes a full year to grow out? I honestly have never in my whole life seen a set of bangs take so long to grow. After almost a year she still had issues with stray wispies!

My gift in life is storytelling. I see a good story and love to tell it. I don't know how Debbie continues to get herself into these situations, but she provides me with some of my best material. Not only that, she provided our church with one of their funniest memories EVER.

Just Debbie...

You have heard the saying "Don't judge a book by its cover." I think "Don't judge a girl by her hair, her clothes, or her jewelry" is equally wise, and kind. Many of us begin working on our outsides for a little pick-me-up when we are down or troubled; we try a new hairdo, redecorate our house, or go out for some good old retail therapy. The myth we are buying into is that if we look good on the outside, it will fix how we feel on the inside. If that doesn't work, we can always stop and pick up some ice cream or other junk food on the way home from the mall.

The context of this verse on adornment in I Peter 3:3 makes it really interesting. This passage is talking about relationships and begins by telling us that our husbands can be won for God without a word. That amazing feat can be accomplished by just our conduct.

I Peter 3:4 goes on to say, "Rather let it be the hidden person of the heart, with the incorruptible beauty of a gentle and quiet spirit, which is very precious in the sight of God" (NKJV). This chapter centers on one very unpopular word to most of us: submission. Submission is voluntarily cooperating with someone out of love and respect for them. It is putting their needs ahead of your own. It is an AGAPE kind of love.

It has been said that a man's greatest need is respect, and a woman's greatest need is love. Interestingly, these are both just opposite sides of the same coin. What really makes someone lovely in our eyes? We may see their beautiful smile or silky hair, but what is it that truly connects us? The answer is very simple. We are all looking for someone who sees us as priceless in their eyes. We need to know that we are special and loved. We were born with that innate desire.

If you think back over any fight you have ever had with your spouse, a family member, or a friend, what was at the center of your disagreement? What was the real issue? When something goes wrong, it is not really the details we are fighting about. The underlying issue is that we somehow feel disrespected, forgotten, abandoned, or unloved. The next step is that we begin to look at alternatives to protect ourselves from being hurt again. We may close ourselves off, fight back, or seek revenge. We may just walk away or end that relationship entirely.

I Peter 3:8-9 provides the answer for any bad day, "Summing up: Be agreeable, be sympathetic, be loving, be compassionate, be humble. That goes for all of you, no exceptions. No retaliation. No sharp-tongued sarcasm. Instead, bless—that's your job, to bless. You'll be a blessing and also get a blessing" (The Message).

Instead of reacting in the flesh, we are to be a blessing. Can you think of a time that your spouse has hurt your feelings? Did it really help to go get a manicure or nice outfit? Well, it probably made you feel better for the moment until you had to pay for it, but it did not fix your aching heart or the part of your relationship that really needed some healing. The only thing able to turn that situation around comes from inward adornment which is a quiet and gentle spirit that returns a blessing.

As women, we have a tough time maintaining healthy self-esteem. When our bangs go awry, we do too. We are constantly surrounded by magazines, television, and movies that tell us to mimic and aspire to Hollywood beauty. If Hollywood's standard is the answer to true happiness, why is it the center of drug abuse, alcoholism, and divorce? They seem to have everything, but what they have is never enough. Our self-esteem has got to last beyond our latest bad haircut, thoughtless remark, or outfit for the day.

Not only do we see divorce on the rise at the same rate in the church as it is in the world, we see that people are simply disconnected from their church and from having healthy friendships. People connect through surfing the web, text, Twitter, and Facebook, but they are more leery than ever about making personal relationships and staying in them. All of the social media make it too easy to walk away when discord erupts.

God has taught me an important lesson about relationships through my friendship with Denise. Denise is an accountant, which means that most of her week is spent on (what I think of as) the wrong side of her brain. She stays immersed in facts and numbers all day. But when she leaves work, she crosses a bridge that allows her access to go back and forth between logic and feelings. I find it very impressive because my bridge does not ever reach the numbers neighborhood. This is sad, but true.

One weekend I was talking to right-brained Denise. She was talking about how she wanted to leave work at noon the following Friday and get away just to play. We're talking about a lazy river, chick flick, and dinner out. She was worn out from work and just wanted to leave it all behind. We had come up with a great plan and we were both excited about it.

When Friday came, I had lined-up someone to stay with my daughter, filled my car with gas, and stood in the long line at the bank so I could make this get-away happen. Denise, however, returned to her office after our conversation and crossed back over her bridge into numbers land. She obviously closed and locked the gate on her bridge because when noon came on Friday, no bells went off. There were no alarms, no sense of something missing – there was nothing. Nada! She was in full work mode.

By five p.m. on the day we had planned to have our girls' get-away, she was grocery shopping and doing whatever else she needed to do. In fact, she even sent me a text during that time to say that she was out doing a little shopping. She asked, "What are you doing?"

I did not text back and say, "I am waiting for you to return to your right mind." In fact, I did not even respond honestly with, "Well, I am sitting here with my feelings a little hurt because it sure feels like you forgot me today." If I had told her the truth, our girls' outing might have been salvaged, but I never mentioned a word. This was my mistake.

My guys were headed out to eat and shop at a big sporting store about an hour's drive away. Golf shopping is not my idea of a fun Friday night, but I thought going to eat was better than sitting home sulking, so I went. But my heart was sad. I felt forgotten, unimportant, and overlooked. I did not mention it to the guys. It was just a girl thing. We get our feelings hurt now and then probably because we are aware that we *have* feelings, but that's a subject for another discussion.

I have to say that my son is a wise old soul in a young man's body. He looked at me and said, "Mom, what's wrong? You look sad. Are you alright?"

He was the only person I chose to tell about this matter as he sincerely asked. I simply said, "I was supposed to do something with Denise today. I guess she just forgot me."

He looked at me with his big smile and said, "Denise could never forget you," and he gave me a big hug. Is this son of mine as wise as King Solomon, or what? This kid has discernment beyond his years. A light went on in my little brain: Denise had forgotten something on her calendar; she had not intentionally forgotten me.

During my long ride home from the big sports store outing, Denise sent me another text. By that time I told her what had happened and that my feelings were hurt. She felt really bad, which made me feel worse. I began to think about what her day was probably like and about how I could not stand her job for even two minutes. Think: high pressure. And then amp that up a few more notches!

I began to think of all of the ways she has blessed my life and that if those blessings could be counted in dollars (her world), my bank account would be overflowing. The thought hit me, *if she never did anything for me for the rest of my life, I am blessed beyond words.* She has been an unconditional friend to me. I am good *as is*. There is nothing I need. Our friendship is enough ... simply enough.

The truth is I forget things all the time. Multiple times she has been with me when I have lost my cell phone, my purse, my car, and (almost) my mind. Did I really have a leg to stand on being upset that she forgot something (namely me)? No! And if I did have a leg to stand on, I would have probably misplaced it, too.

A best friend is someone you cannot stay angry with for very long because you would miss them too much. A best friend is someone who, at the age of fifty, will walk into a Wal-Mart in broad daylight just to buy a pregnancy test for their (fifty-something) friend who is hiding out in the car. That is a true friend! A real friend is big enough to apologize to you when you probably need to apologize to them. Every true friend is a little glimpse of God. They leave footprints on our hearts, and are TLC for our souls.

When you have a bad hair day, a bad friendship day, or a rough day in your marriage, remember this: God loves you unconditionally. He will never forget you, even though it may seem He is late. He not only loves you but He sees the inward beauty of your spirit. He counts every hair on your head and He knows every need you have before it is ever spoken.

There is an interesting parable which exemplifies this very issue. Jesus tells the story of a man with a debt that he could not pay. His master cancelled the man's debt and let him go. Matthew 18:28-32 goes on to tell us that this forgiven man then found his fellow servant and he grabbed him and choked him demanding to be paid back for the money the servant owed him. The master then called him a "wicked servant" because after receiving grace, he had turned around and showed unforgiveness to his debtor. The man was thrown in prison, and the Bible ends this story with a daunting thought: those that receive forgiveness from God but are not willing to forgive others will receive punishment verses forgiveness. Ouch, that thought is a show stopper!

Through grace, we can cut our family, friends, neighbors, and church some slack – a lot of slack actually – because we need grace, too. We can reach out and love others even when we feel hurt, overlooked, or unimportant. We can reset the thermostat of our hearts and give love in spite of our feelings. The Bible simply says that love covers a multitude of sins. I have a multitude of sins that need covering; therefore I have a lot of forgiving to do.

Has someone in your life hurt your feelings? When you choose to simply forgive and cover the offense with love, your relationship will begin to grow again.

Take it from "Sista Moe" of the "Three Stooges," I look wayyyyyy better with my bangs, and we all look much better when we are sporting a face that is adorned with love.

Tubular Therapy Thought

Do you know the good thing about a bad hair day? Your hair grows back and you move on ... When you choose to love and give grace to others you are set Freeeeeee!

CHAPTER NINE

A Near Miss

*(A GPS can be a wonderful thing, unless it puts you on a
dark mountain road on a dark, dangerous, rainy night. If
and when that happens you will need A A A—"An Angel
Army". That is exactly what we needed and received.)*

*"I have heard your cry and have come to rescue you. Now,
take off your shoes for this is Holy Ground." (God)
"Who am I to go for you?" (Moses)
"I AM and I will be with you" ... (God)
(Short summary of Exodus 3)*

Funny Denise...

Ever walked into a place and thought, *"OK ... once I walk out of here I am going to know which way I am going and how to get there."* Then you walk out and wonder if you could be any more confused than you are already?

That is what happened to me when I left a writers' conference recently. I walked out wondering if all the work we had accomplished in writing was for nothing. We were told we had a "hit" on our hands, and that it was a great concept, but we were also told the hardest part is the next step and we didn't have anything we needed to get there.

I prayed, *"God, did you bring us this far to abandon us now?"*

Debbie and I were both exhausted, so we decided to get massages and eat somewhere before our 2 ½ hour drive home. We tried multiple places to eat in San Diego, but on a Saturday night there was nothing but great smelling food and long lines. We ended up at a fast food restaurant and began to talk about the writers' conference.

I had thought I would walk in and those publishers would shout from the rooftop, "Where have you been? I have been waiting 30 years for you to write your book!!" There would be people trying to get my attention and I would have to sit back and make a decision. Instead, I walked in to find no bells going off, no whistles sounding, no applause ... absolutely nothing but a lot of well-dressed, brilliant writers. It was overwhelming, but had God placed me there?

Debbie came up with a plan for our book and I was on board immediately. After an hour long dinner I was feeling somewhat better, but I could tell she wanted to be home and the thought of driving after dark on rain-drenched, foggy roads was bothering her.

We turned on the GPS and off we drove. About two minutes into the drive Debbie started the conversation with, "Now you aren't taking us through the **mountains**, right? I don't want to go through the **mountains.** You need to find a different route if we are going through the **Mountains.** I don't feel safe in the **MOUNTAINS!**"

All I heard was ...

"Mountains ... Mountains ... MOUNTAINS are **BAD!**"

I assured her that the GPS was not taking us through the mountains, "We are only 12.8 miles away from Interstate 8. We are going on known highways and no mountain roads."

Mountain roads are named after trees, animals, or old dead guys, I thought to myself. This was actually a highway we were going to be on for about nine miles. So I promised her we were fine and no mountains.

As we began to climb what I assumed was a small hill, I soon realized that this highway I had her on was, indeed, heading UP and it was extremely curvy. Debbie lost all sense of humor.

I wanted to remind her that it wasn't my fault. Her GPS had led us astray before (remember the railroad tracks in San Diego?). So, as you can see, this GPS was prone to make mistakes. She wasn't in any mood to hear excuses.

I thought in my easy going way that I would just make small talk to ease the tension. We would talk about the weather ... the drizzly, foggy, cold, dark weather. I thought twice about that and decided against it. So I began to let her know that even though we *seemed* to be in the mountains, that it might feel that way because it was dark out and we just couldn't see that we were actually very close to the interstate that would take us home. I then began aloud to count down the miles to the turnoff for the Interstate ... 9.8 miles ... pause ... 9.7 miles ... pause ... 9.6 miles ...

At 9.4 miles she shot me a look that made me think she was rethinking why she had brought me along on this trip. I decided to only update the mileage every 2 miles – another bad move on my part. God asked me nicely to shut my mouth (glad it was God and not Debbie at that point!)

As we approached an intersection, I remembered having seen that we were supposed to make a turn, but wasn't sure which way. I glanced down at the GPS I had snugly tucked in my hands (felt I was safer holding it than giving Debbie a chance to chuck it at me), but the GPS suddenly shut down. Strange … it was plugged into the car's power outlet. I quickly turned it back on and began reprogramming it.

Debbie was in the left lane and began to make a left turn when I shouted, "No … No … No!! Turn right, Dude!"

I felt God once again telling me, "Hush up sweet thing." So I just stared at the GPS praying it was going to say turn left and all will be OK, but it didn't.

We drove for about a mile before I finally said, "You need to turn left here and we will head back down the hill."

She shot back, "It's NOT A HILL … IT'S A MOUNTAIN!"

"OK … well … can you please turn left off this mountain and head down?" I answered.

She got in the turn lane that we could barely see due to the fog, and began to turn left, but there was no road! None! Nada! Zippo! The saving grace was it was pitch dark in the car and I couldn't see the look she was shooting me, but boy howdy, did I know it was a bad one! She immediately banged a U in the road and down the *mountain* we went.

I was going to let her know how close we were to Interstate 8 but thought to myself, *Ah … not such a good idea for me to talk right now.*

God said, "Yep … silence is golden!"

Debbie had played country music for most of the trip, but the minute we were headed up the mountain, she had changed the CD to praise music. Now, I would like to say that I am a fabulous singer, but God has told me not to lie in times of trouble, so you should know I can't carry a tune in a bucket. But on this particular road I was humming softly with the song playing and praying for the drizzle and heavy fog to end.

I was staring at the GPS (to avoid Debbie's drop dead looks) and noticed that her speed had dropped from 40 to 20 miles an hour. We were on a straight road and I was going to say something, but by this time God had brought out the duct tape and was waving it, oh so gently, in front of my face … so I kept quiet.

And then it happened. We came around a sharp curve on this two-lane mountain road. Our vision ahead was further obscured by a pile of rocks that came right up to the side of the road, and covering our side of the road and part of the oncoming traffic was an SUV, upside down with smoke billowing out of it. Glass was everywhere, along with pieces of the vehicle. I screamed and Debbie softly said, "God help us!"

She swerved around the vehicle and it was like *s-l-o-w m-o-t-i-o-n,* but we made it safely. The next 6 ½ miles were driven in silence. I'm not sure when it started, but soon both of us were singing at the top of our lungs "Bless the Lord oh my soul!" It didn't even matter that I couldn't sing; we both were just praising God.

Just Debbie...

We live in a three dimensional world ... length, breadth, and height. Yet, the Bible is filled with stories of a different dimension. This realm remains beyond our limited human understanding. There are stories of a donkey talking, a chariot flying, and an entire Red Sea parting. There are bushes in flames that never burn up, and three men tossed into a furnace where a fourth man appears with them in the inferno. None of God's people were harmed in this intense fire, but wouldn't it be amazing to hear what they discussed in the fiery furnace?

Some amazing dimensional defying moments were when Jesus walked through a door, Peter joined Jesus walking on the water, and Elijah left this life riding in a chariot without facing death. This entire realm of thinking is beyond our normal experiences, senses, or understanding. Yet, we know that these small glimpses are just a taste of the fourth dimension where God resides. He is not limited by time, space, or eternity. He is omnipotent, omnipresent, omniscient, which means that He is sovereign over life and death.

God knows all, has power over everything, and is never surprised by our human failings. He *will* accomplish His ultimate goal, and He uses all of our strengths and weaknesses for His greater plans and purposes. There are moments when we, as humans, catch a glimpse of this fourth dimension, and – just as Denise and I experienced on that dark and scary mountain road – those brief moments never fail to leave us speechless and humbled.

One example of this is the story of Moses which is recorded for us in the third chapter of Exodus. Moses was a man with fears and failures. The Bible does not hide his failings from us; instead, it actually tells us that God chose to use a man who had killed an Egyptian, who was harming one of the Israelites. Moses lost his temper and committed murder, but God never lost sight of His greater purpose for Moses' life. One of the most amazing stories found in the Bible is Moses' encounter with God.

What is truly incredible is that Moses is one of very few people to have ever been *in the very presence of God*, on more than one occasion. Moses had an encounter with God at a burning bush. He was tending the flock for his father-in-law ... it was just an ordinary day. Exodus 3:2 tells us that an angel of the Lord appeared to Moses from within a bush that appeared to be on fire, but the bush did not burn up. Instead, God spoke through the flaming bush. Exodus 3:4 goes on to say, "When the Lord saw that he had gone over to look, God called to him from within the bush, 'Moses, Moses'!" And Moses said, "Here I am" (NIV).

God told Moses to take off his sandals because the place he was standing was holy ground. He hid his face because he was afraid to look at God. He began to explain to Moses the bigger picture because He had heard Moses' cries and He knew the suffering of His people. God was ready to rescue them and He wanted to use Moses.

Moses' response was basically, "Who am I that you would use me?" God's message to Moses was simply this, "I will be with you."

God appeared to Moses while he was tending the sheep. How ordinary and humdrum is that? God's mere presence changed a normal day into something supernaturally powerful! Can you begin to imagine going about your normal, ordinary, humdrum everyday business and encountering God's actual powerful presence? Does the bush still burn today?

Is it possible for us to actually experience God's intervening presence in our lives today? Does God ever say to us, "I have heard your cry and I am getting ready to rescue you and your loved ones"?

Each and every day when we thank God for our food before we eat, we are really saying that we believe His *providence* in our lives. When we ask for His *protection* before we head out in our vehicle and when our children walk out the door to go to school, we are seeking His divine protection over our lives and the lives of our loved ones. Each night we pray and thank Him for the day He has given us. We ask for His will to be done on earth as it is in Heaven. We end these prayers with, "In Jesus' name, Amen." We are *proclaiming* His sovereignty and the power that comes to us through merely speaking the name of Jesus, acknowledging that everything we have comes from Him. We are also being reminded in these prayers that *it is not about us*. It is *all* about Him.

But the question remains: where is fear in this whole providence, protection, and proclamation scenario? Can we truly plan for our own strength, success, or safety?

Prayer is a funny thing. We pour out all of our burdens to God and ask Him a million and one questions, and His answers are always resounding and direct, even in His silence. He always answers the real questions of our heart. He gives us clear direction and simply says, "This is the way. Walk in it." The rest is faith.

It felt like God had been pouring out His Spirit and blessings into my life prior to this writers' conference. His Word had literally become alive daily to me. Wherever I went, whatever I did, ideas and creativity just flowed out of me like water pouring over Niagara Falls. I would pray and hand over my concerns to God, releasing them to Him before going to sleep in peace each night. I would awaken with clarity replacing confusion each morning, as new thoughts, ideas, and directions would lead me another step down the road.

But at the conference, I seriously began to doubt. I could hear Moses' words echoing, *Why me? Who am I to sell a book? I am a no-body.*

I began to pray and ask God how we could know which way to proceed with all of the confusing information we had just gathered about publishing our books. I had tons of questions, but no answers. I felt pretty discouraged. So, I told God all of my concerns and prayed that He would give us a miraculous answer, thinking perhaps some publishing company would just mysteriously call.

Instead, in response to my prayer, I got a very strong prompting: *Do this differently than the world does. Take your **first book** (Happy Dance) and offer them to Me by giving the first group of them away to people that really need them.* I pictured hospitals, women's retreats, people with cancer, and special needs families. I saw the faces of people who needed encouragement and to "find their smile" again. They could laugh at the funny stories and then be reminded that God fights fear with friendship and faith.

This strong intervening thought wasn't the direction I was expecting, but it was the direction I truly needed. I shared this prompting with Denise over dinner, and she was on board immediately! We would choose to give our writing to God and walk in faith trusting Him to provide for us. And at the time of this writing, over 2,000 books have been given away so far; our first fruits!

Guess what came immediately after our decision to trust God? We found ourselves on that dark, misty, foggy mountain road! Choosing to follow God's leading in faith never comes without a trial, a test, and a time of triumph when we walk in His WILL!

As Denise told you, our drive home from the writers' conference was the scariest car ride I can recall. It was dark, misty, and very foggy. We quickly found ourselves on one of the most dangerous mountain roads with extremely poor road conditions. I was wishing I was on a different route altogether.

This was NOT good. In fact, I had *a very bad, unsettled feeling!* Then, we lost our GPS service completely.

I couldn't just sit at the intersection, so I turned – the wrong way – taking us up the mountain. After about a mile, realizing we should have gone the other direction, we turned around to head back to the intersection. Due to the fog, we couldn't see the road in front of us, so we were traveling about 10 miles under the speed limit. As we came around a bend we could not see much of anything. As Denise told you, she wondered at the time why I had slowed down to about 20 miles per hour ... I had no idea.

Contrary to Denise's joking comments in this story, to tell you the truth I really wasn't even paying much attention to her. I was terrified, praying, and feeling like something was very wrong; my spirit felt a strong warning!

Denise would admit to me later that although she was trying to stay calm and talk to me, she too had the very same feeling. At one point she saw a vision that was surprising and unforgettable. She saw a glimpse of two coffins and it frightened her. This happened before we came upon the next sight.

If we had turned the right direction to begin with, we would have been at the location of the accident at about the time it occurred. For some reason, beyond my understanding, without any conscious decision to do so, I had slowed down for no apparent reason. If I had been going the speed limit, there would have been no avoiding that accident in the fog. As we watched about twelve emergency vehicles heading up the hill, we knew we had experienced "A Near Miss".

If our eyes had been opened to see the other realm that night, I wonder if we would have seen a host of angels? The one thing we both knew with all certainty is that God intervened in our lives on that frightful mountain road. It still gives us chills.

Whenever a dark, foggy, stormy night happens in our lives, our visibility goes to zero. We cannot see, and we cannot understand. We can only listen to the crowd of experts, look at a long list of fearful possibilities, or check a man-made GPS. If you have ever used a GPS, you know how wonderful it is when it works and how frustrating it can be when it directs you onto a dark and dangerous mountain road.

We often use the phrase "as fate would have it," or we call something a coincidence. But the Bible tells us of a sovereign God who holds all things in His hands. God, alone, knows the past, present, and future. He has spoken in the past through His prophets, His Written Word, His only Son, and by His Sprit.

The Bible simply tells us that our God is the same God yesterday, today, and tomorrow. He is unchangeable, unshakeable, and undeniable! We can then live everyday here on earth with the confidence that we serve a God who not only speaks, but lovingly intervenes in our lives. He holds all things in His hands. Our God is the Lord over life, death, and eternity. He has the ability to bring good, even out of bad. With this confidence, perhaps we should stop spending our time on earth fearing death. Instead, we should simply live each day in light of Heaven.

Many of us spend our entire lives fearing death rather than living life full-throttle with faith. Unless God allows it, no mountain road can take us; the enemy can't defeat us. We are not going anywhere until God is ready to say to us, "Welcome home good and faithful servant. Enter into your rest."

I was reminded that there was no "near miss" that night while on our dark, foggy mountain road. I sensed God's Spirit speaking to my heart, saying, "I AM THAT I AM. I will be with you." No, this was no "near miss". This was another dimension entirely. This was the dimension where angels speak and faith triumphs over fear.

This very night was when we became "the barefoot authors". We have seen the bush and it still burns today. The God of Moses is still the "Great I AM". Our shoes are off and we stand in humility, faith, and AWE on HOLY GROUND!

Our "Near Miss" is often "God Drawing Near"!

Tubular Therapy Thought

The God of Moses is the same God who intervenes on every dark, foggy, dangerous mountain road that we travel. He hears your soft whispered prayer, "God help me!" One simple prayer of faith can transport your feet from the hum-drum and ordinary onto Holy Ground!

CHAPTER TEN

What's Important

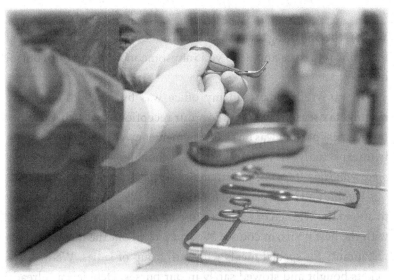

*(Never and I mean EVER let a Mediclinic (Doc in the Box)
do a surgery on you...unless you are writing a
book and you need some new material!!)*

*"Love the Lord your God with all your heart, and with all
your soul, with all your strength, and with all your mind;
and 'love your neighbor as yourself'."*
--Luke 10:27 (NIV)

Funny Denise...

What is the one thing that can pull you out of your own little world of insignificant issues and drop you into someone else's out-of-control life?

It was Wednesday and my office was buzzing. Phones were ringing, tax season was upon me, our receptionist was on vacation, my business partner was on a family emergency, clients were dropping in unexpectedly – it was a nightmare. I thought, *why, oh why does my office – and life – turn into pure chaos when I just want to go on a vacation?*

Debbie and I had planned for months this long weekend getaway to attend the Women of Faith conference. We had arranged the hotel with the best pools, of course! We had picked out the most fabulous restaurants for special meals with our group of ladies. We had our tickets bought and stowed safely in our purses. Debbie was already packed as usual. I just figured I would buy news clothes – it's just easier!) Debbie had prepared meals and arranged them neatly in the freezer for quick thawing and cooking; I had left money on the kitchen table for fast food. As you can tell, Debbie and I do family life a little differently. She's a mom and I'm a 'Wanna- Be'. We were set and ready to go.

The deal was that we were both keeping secrets. Debbie's secret was a growth on her arm that had been hurting for almost 3 months. I had noticed her bandage but Debbie is an avid gardener so I just assumed she had gotten scratched or pricked while gardening. I, too, consider myself an avid gardener. The difference in our styles of gardening is she waters and cares for her plants; I plant them, water them once and hope for the best. Hers last for several months; mine look beautiful for several hours – as we live in the desert.

My secret was a lump in my armpit I had discovered about a week before the trip. Every day I looked at it, every day I was in denial.

This particular day Debbie's arm was really hurting and, after a bit of prodding (more like threatening) on my part, she consented to go see what we so fondly refer to as the "doc-in-the-box." You know the type you can just drop in and they immediately see you, no appointment necessary.

I had gone to work that morning not thinking about anything but the mounds of paperwork on my desk. I heard the door of my office open and shut, and Debbie appeared in my doorway. I was in the middle of what I thought was a major crisis, so I asked her to sit down and I would be done in just a minute or two.

As I was calculating, I realized she was there almost an hour before we were supposed to go to lunch, and as I looked up to see her face I quickly surmised that I should have looked up sooner.

The tears began to fall and her voice began to quiver, "They want to cut it out and send it off to pathology."

My heart sunk. My brain kicked in and all I said was, "It will be alright. It's gonna be alright ... trust me."

All of a sudden, my work wasn't so important, the phones didn't matter, and the clients could wait. All that was important was my friend was hurting and scared.

After much discussion, Debbie decided to have the doc-in-the-box remove the lesion (that's what a doctor calls something when they don't exactly know what it is ... isn't that just peachy keen?)

Now remember, Debbie has a phobia of doctors, hospitals, needles, blood...all of those things that are needed for healing. But after a very long, drawn out conversation at lunch, she decided that she would go that afternoon. She knew I was busy so she said I didn't need to come, but that was a moot point. She didn't have a vote in it. I got to the doc-in-the-box a little after 4:00 pm and marched past the receptionist and nurses at the front. I then proceeded to knock on doors all the way down the hall until I got the right one. I finally found Debbie standing next to her son.

I said, "Hey, sit on the patient chair."

"NOPE," was her reply, "I think I'll stand."

"Listen, Spunky," I said, "You need to sit your little self down and relax. It's going to be quick and painless and we are here for you."

Finally, she agreed. Then the nurse came in and said there could only be one person in the room with her. I gave her son the look of doom, so he slumped out of the room and down the hall to the waiting area.

I talked and talked about everything I could think of to keep her mind off her situation. In walked two nurses (I use that term loosely). What happened next was like watching Tweedle Dee and Tweedle Dum. They began to prepare for the procedure by taking out each item the doctor needed. It wouldn't have been so bad, but not only did they hold up each item, announce it and what it was for, but they placed it on a table right in front of Debbie. The play-by-play went something like this ...

Tweedle Dee starts, "First comes the scissors – used to cut the stitches. Next is the second pair of scissors used to cut away any loose skin. Here is the needle used to give the shot into the lesion to deaden the area. Next is the scalpel used to slice and dice the affected area. Last comes a digger (for lack of a better term) used to dig out the lesion."

Obviously this was a training session for the Tweedle sisters as their incompetence was shining like the noonday sun on a southern California desert in the month of July.

Debbie was looking at the utensils, and then looking at me. I would smile, but it was that crooked smile, you know the one you use when the waitress asks you how you like the Brussel sprouts and you respond with, "Oh yes, I love them!" while your throat is closing up in rebellion.

The doctor arrived on the scene and announced that he would be creating a sterile area and to not come in contact with it. He laid a paper napkin on a tray, placed her arm on the tray, and placed another napkin with a hole in it over Debbie's arm. *Yep, yep, yep ... that's a sterile area if I ever saw one.*

I was told not to approach the area as apparently I wasn't sterile. I wanted to respond, "Yes, sir, I am sterile! I had a hysterectomy 11 years ago and am probably more sterile than you!" But I didn't feel this was any place for levity ... and he didn't seem to be the type who had cracked a smile in years.

I kept my eye on Debbie as they began the procedure. At first her eyes were open but then something happened. It was like watching a train wreck in slow motion. The doctor took on the persona of Howard Cosell and began to give a play-by-play of the action that was occurring. He began to show Debbie how small the needle was that he was going to stick in the lesion to make it numb. He told her how he would wiggle it around to freeze the area. Then as he was cutting her arm he told her that the first time he ever cut skin was on a cadaver.

I watched the color drain from Debbie's face and she began to hold her breath. I thought, *yep ... two things are about to happen: she is going to pass out and she is going to throw up!* I just didn't know which would be first.

He continued with his rousing rendition of, "I am the best doctor in the world," telling us how this lesion had deep roots and he was having to pull and tug to get it all out. By this time, I was ready to slap him silly. He had finally stopped talking (I hoped to concentrate on what he was doing) when, lo-and-behold, the ditzy nurse began to ask him questions about the procedure, and we were back in the saddle again!

I knew it was a matter of moments before Debbie would be slumped on the floor. She started wiping the sweat off her forehead and Tweedle Dee finally came to her senses and realized this arm is attached to an actual living patient, who was losing it, big time!

They finally noticed her slumping down and asked if she was OK. She weakly responded, "No." They laid her chair back and asked me to hold her legs up in the air.

I knew there was a reason for that, and maybe if I had paid more attention in anatomy class in school, I would have known why they asked me to do it, but I was a little distracted at that particular moment. I thought he just wanted me to move her leg to the side, so I did. The doctor motioned for me to lift her leg higher, so I raised it about an inch. He finally gave me a look of disgust and said, "PICK UP HER LEG IN THE AIR!"

Now, the average bear would have picked up both legs, but not me. I picked up one leg and held it there ... wondering ... pondering ... I thought to myself, *what in God's green earth is the reason for this leg lifting exercise in the middle of this procedure?* So I lowered it ... then lifted it ... then lowered it ... then lifted it.

Finally the doctor looked at me and said, "HOLD IT UP!"

I said, "The whole time, dude?"

"Yes," he replied.

So, there I stood in the "sterile area" holding up her leg. He looked at me and said, "Both legs need to be up in the air."

"Ohhhh," I said, "Both legs, huh?"

He shook his head to indicate what he meant, so I grabbed the other leg and lifted.

Little did I realize until I heard the scissors, the scalpel, the needle, and the digger hit the floor that, apparently, her leg was under the "sterile area" and I had just made the area unsterile, to say the least. But, oh baby, I had those legs doing the Jane Fonda of lifting.

The doctor began to stitch Debbie's arm. I watched him make the first stitch and tie it off; then he made the second stitch, and tied it off. I was good ... no queasy feeling for me ... no siree, Bob! The nurse was still fanning Debbie and I was still doing the Jane Fonda with her legs, while watching him to make sure he did it all OK. But then, he went to stitch the middle part.

He pushed the needle through her skin. It popped through the first side, and as he pushed it through the other side, he spoke the words you should never hear your doctor say.

"Oops … I don't think I like that stitch." He backed it out and did it again, over and over. Every time it made a weird popping sound. The third time my lights were going out. I thought, *if I hit the floor who is going to lift my legs to do the Jane Fonda?* I held it together for Debbie's sake and she managed to hold all of her bodily fluids inside, for mine.

The afternoon certainly ended a lot differently than I had envisioned when my day began. My world was normally filled with piles of papers, numbers, projects, and deadlines. God had redirected me to see a person in need of my attention that day.

That same lesson was brought home to me, again, as I thought back on the medical team that was there to treat Debbie and bring healing. They were looking at her arm but they had entirely missed seeing HER, right there in front of them.

Sometimes what seems urgent is really not what is most important. This is called "The Tyranny of the Urgent." What seems to be so pressing can sometimes rob us of what is most valuable in our lives. I had to wonder how many other days I was a lot like that little medical team, busily working on my project but missing the bigger picture.

I went to bed that night reflecting on the people in my life who are so dear to me. Sometimes I simply miss them … my husband, my son, my parents, my friends.

Then it hit me, *there are days that I even miss seeing God!*

I could picture Him sitting in His chair just waiting for me to look up.

Just Debbie...

Do you ever just feel like an arm on a tray? These days we get on the phone and call for assistance from our bank, our internet company, or just about any business, and we hear something like, "Press #1 if you want a live person, Press #2 if you actually want someone who lives in your country. Go ahead and press #3 as that's not going to happen! Before I can put you through, I need the last four digits of your social security number. You must also submit your password; now subtract your pin number and divide by your three digit code."

Without consulting AAA, or scheduling your airfare or hotel, you have landed in a third world country. It's a trip alright!

Does anyone actually remember Dr. Marcus Welby, Dr. Quinn, or Dr. Huxtable? Perhaps you may remember when Michael J. Fox played Doc Hollywood and whose little sports car broke down in a small town? He could not wait to get out of there to get to the big city, but he found himself falling in love with all of the people in that little community. One family could not afford to pay him, so they gave him his very own pig which he took for daily walks. Can you imagine living back in the day when a doctor actually made house calls? Doc Hollywood did ... with pig in hand. You've just got to love a show like that.

We live in a day where we are a number, a claim, or a client. If someone in a faraway land decides to approve our number, then we may move on to receive what we need. As Denise described, I was pretty much "an arm on a tray" in the clinic that day. Not only that, but after it was over, I asked the doctor a question and his response showed no care or respect for me as a person. Have you ever felt like an "issue" instead of a person?

The Bible tells the story of a woman with a bleeding issue who reached out and touched the hem of Jesus' coat without uttering a word. We don't even know her name; she was just an issue, part of a faceless mob, until she encountered the Messiah that day. What did He see when He looked at her? Did He see a mess, an inconvenience in His busy day, or an interruption to His speaking circuit? One more person who needed something?

Listen to her situation as found in Luke 8:43 "And a woman was there who had been subject to bleeding for **twelve years**, but no one could heal her" (NIV). Did you catch the length of her problem? This woman had been unclean, unhealed, and unnoticed for **TWELVE** long years. That is suffering. There was no hope in site. That is until she caught site of Jesus, the Messiah, and the Healer, who was the Son of God.

The Bible tells us that Jesus looked right at her and called her daughter. He saw a woman of faith and He told her that her faith had healed her. You notice that in this story it was not Jesus' busy schedule that dictated His behavior. His mission, His calling, and her need, were all that motivated Him that day. He looked at her with eyes of love and saw a woman who simply believed. She came ... she touched ... she received. If that were not enough, out of love and concern for her as a person, He took extra time to acknowledge her even in her desperation. He could have walked on, letting her think she had taken something she – and many others – may have felt she didn't deserve. But He wanted to reassure her that it was OK, that she had received the precious gift of healing from Him because she had the simple faith to make that brave gesture.

This all brings us back to our opening question: What is really important, and what is the difference between the urgent and the important? Jesus only had three years of ministry to turn the world upside down. Yet, He took time for this woman with an unclean, unmentionable problem, and before everyone there, He acknowledged her as worthy.

Do we realize that every time God gets ready to move, He calls someone to put their papers down, look up from their work, and move for Him? The legacy of our lives will be charted in these ordinary, easily overlooked moments. It will be in these times of need that we will say, "I see a person here." I choose to minister to a person that is in need.

Many years ago, I was standing at my keyboard leading worship on a Sunday morning. As I was looking out over the audience, I felt a prompting to go back and talk to a woman sitting on the back row. As we continued to sing, I continued to struggle with this thought. *Where had this thought come from, why was it so strong, and why was I to do this right now?*

After we finished, I walked back there, knelt down by her and said something to the effect of, "How are you doing today?" This lady burst into tears and bolted out of the auditorium. I quickly followed after her. She asked me why I had asked her that. I told her I didn't know; I just felt that I was supposed to be there. She told me she had just found out she had cancer that week.

I cannot tell you how glad I am that on that particular day, I had seen the person, not just the arm. On that day, like Denise, I had simply looked up and left the "necessity of the urgent" behind. When I responded, without understanding why I was to go, I got to see what was really important.

When God interrupts our busy day, He is intervening to bring about a blessing in our lives and in the lives of others. Galatians 6:10 (AMP) says it like this, "Be mindful to be a blessing". Being mindful is an intentional act on our part. It requires seeing and choosing the important over the urgent.

As we sit at our desk or go about our daily business will we merely see "the arm" or the whole person? Will we be lost in the urgent or take time for the important? Will we be truly mindful to be a blessing in the lives of those around us this day?

Tubular Therapy Thought

*Just being there...loving God and others...
that's what is most important. Only that which
is done for others in the name of Jesus will last
for all time and eternity!*

REFLECTIONS

"Gone Tubular?"

"Dear friends, since God so loved us, we also ought to love one another. No one has ever seen God; but if we love each other, God lives in us, and his love is made complete in us ... There is no fear in love. But perfect love drives out fear, because fear has to do with punishment. The one who fears is not made perfect in love."

—*I John 4:11, 12; 18 (NIV)*

Just Debbie...

Many years ago I was teaching a Women's Bible Study and I read James 5:16 to the ladies. It says, *"Confess your sins to each other and pray for each other so that you may be healed. The prayer of a righteous person is powerful and effective"* (NIV).

One of the ladies in that study was not too happy with me, at all. She looked at me and said, "Are you saying that we have to confess our sins aloud to other people?"

I replied, "I am just reading from God's Word."

I had to agree with her that I don't personally get the "warm fuzzies" about every one of God's commands. God allows each of us to choose whether we will obey and receive His healing. Sometimes it is tough – really tough. But when we trust and obey we are always blessed in this life and the one to come.

I must admit that I understand her frustration. Somewhere along the line, she probably trusted someone and ended up being hurt. Someone might have judged her, gossiped about her, or just walked away without caring, listening, or loving. I completely understand all the risks of friendship and accountability.

Sometimes churches, families, and friendships can be dangerous places for wounded souls. If that has happened to you, I am truly sorry. My heart breaks for you, for me, and for our God whom we ALL let down when we react without love.

There is a story in the Old Testament that overflows with heartbreak because of a relationship that went wrong, very wrong. This is a story of three men that God loved. Saul, David, and Jonathan were the three strands of a cord that should not have been broken, if they had stood together. David was a young man with a pure heart who faithfully served King Saul and became best friends with Saul's son, Jonathan. What a tight little cord, right?

When Saul was filled with anxiety, David would play soothing music to calm Saul's spirit. There was genuine love and affection between them. God had chosen David to be the next king, and he was also the brave and faithful warrior who slew the giant, Goliath. When the people began to sing David's praise, Saul became jealous. In the days to come, Saul was more interested in hating David than in loving his own son, Jonathan. Although David was Jonathan's best friend, and Saul's faithful servant and comforter, Saul was simply filled with jealousy and rage towards David. Saul lost his kingdom and family because of pride, jealousy, and unforgiveness. He actually sent his men out to try and kill David. Now that is an example of a love/hate relationship if I have ever seen one.

Saul was oblivious to his sin. All he could see was his hurt, his loss, and his pride. David had two choices: he had the opportunity to "bring Saul down" or "to lift God up". David chose the latter, and God exalted him to be the next king.

I wish I could tell you that friendships never go south, but they do; or that whenever you open your heart and share your hurts with someone, you will receive grace. I must admit that, like David, there have been times in the ministry when I have served others and tried to comfort them in their pain, only to have them turn around and act in ways that have harmed my spirit, soul, and immediate future.

We must choose wisely with whom we will float down the lazy rivers of life. We should carefully choose to whom we confess our failings. Those closest to us need to be righteous people whose prayers are powerful and effective.

But when all is said and done, even if you have poured out your love, your comfort, and your friendship, like David, and you find that you are facing a Saul, remember this: God still calls us to confess. God still calls us to love, God still calls us to turn the other cheek, and God still calls us to forgive more times than you can actually count.

Jesus summarized the greatest commandment for us in Matthew 22:17, telling us we are to love God first and others second. There is no greater calling as only faith, hope, and love will go with us into Heaven; everything else will simply be left behind.

This book has been about faith over fear. There is only one way for our faith to triumph. That path is through perfect love. His perfect love is like a big inner tube that surrounds you and keeps you afloat. Not only that, but it is never His desire for us to go solo. That is why He has placed us in a family, His church. He has called us "to bear one another's burdens". Thus the word picture "Tubular Therapy"; we are healed as we simply take Him at His Word and float together through the rapids of life.

God's love is made complete in us every time we repent, apologize first, receive grace, admit our weakness, and accept His strength. What can the enemy do to us when we acknowledge that we are weak but our God is strong?

Have you ever felt like you have been standing at the top of a cliff looking down and the enemy, himself, was presenting each of the temptations? The Bible tells us that Jesus was perfect, but He was tempted in every way, just as we are. I not only believe that, but I can tell you that I have experienced a little taste of those common trials, personally. As I was going through this time, the Word of God spoke to me so strongly.

I felt like I was standing at the very edge of a cliff, looking down. I could hear the enemy calling me, "Just jump; throw yourself down." Then I heard God saying, "No, look up. Never fight the enemy with your own words or strength." Why, oh why did I not just quote the words of scripture and rest in God's peace like Jesus did? I came so close to falling and failing the test.

I need to tell you one very important thing about this whole ordeal. Do you know what kept me from crashing and burning? It was the very same thing that also kept David in line. He had a friend named Jonathan who loved him like a brother, and the Lord God Almighty was his constant companion.

Two years prior to my time of testing I had a very close friend who told of a dream she had about me. In the dream she saw me kneeling on the ground and crying; she said in the dream she felt far away and helpless. I did not understand this dream, but I remembered it with all the details. Two years later, she was praying for me and she gave me a few words about a situation I was facing. Her words were, "Wait, WAIT, *WAIT* ... give it to God."

I wish I could tell you that I locked-in on that warning and missed the large hole that was waiting for me in the middle of my proverbial street. But I did not miss the hole or heed the warning, nor did I walk down a different street. However, as I found myself outside, on my knees, crying out to God I recognized the warning of my friend's dream. I was in the place, position, and surrounded with the colors she had described. In that very moment, it all clicked. God brought to my mind her dream and my warning.

At that moment, I realized, again, that God is sovereign. I can tell you this beyond a shadow of a doubt: my life, ministry, and future were spared from the destruction that the enemy desired for me. I wanted to quit ... to run ... to give-up. That was what the enemy had in mind for me. He can defeat us anytime he can get us to choose fear over faith.

I can tell you this much, there are rapids out there, undercurrents, and huge boulders. Denise is actually correct – the water is not always your friend. We dare not ride through the storms of life without a friend beside us and a tube to keep us afloat.

Our desire through this book was to share with you what God has done in our lives. He did it for us, and He'll do it for you, simply for the asking. As you can see from our stories, we have had quite a few rapids to face; but we have also had a lot to look back and laugh about.

We have both grown stronger in our lives because of the strength that comes with having a *friend that loves at all times and who was born for adversity* as Proverbs 17:17 reminds us. As the Bible says, having a friend divides cares and multiplies joys. Not only that, but when "your lights are going out" you may need someone to help your legs do "the Jane Fonda".

We are committed to floating through life, "Tubular Therapy" style. It is our hope that you have been blessed while floating down life's lazy river with two crazy friends whose fears have been faced with friendship and faith in a great big God!

Let the hurt go and let God's healing come in. It's cleansing. It's healing. It's really pretty amazing. We float awhile and talk awhile. We laugh awhile and cry awhile. And we will all experience God's healing touch. "As iron sharpens iron" we will face our fears together, and when we get our "tushy" out of the floating tube, we will all go home better than we came!

Will you choose today to live a life that is "totally tubular"?

Friendship's Prayer

If you do not have a trustworthy friend, mentor, or prayer partner to encourage you at this time, please don't be discouraged. God is waiting for you to ask Him, and He will provide for you all that you need. Perhaps it is time to quit trying to make things happen on your own, as God always has a much better plan.

Are you afraid, lonely, in need of a hand up? God specializes in *Tubular Therapy*-style unconditional love. He keeps us afloat in troubled times; He is the God of Faith over Fear!

We invite you to pray with us right now …

Dear God,

Come into my life.

Like the woman who reached out to touch Jesus' coat, I need you.

In faith I will put my trust in YOU.

Today I choose faith over fear, healing over heartbreak, and hope over despair.

Thank you, God, that you have placed me into your Church.

Now I have a new family, friends, mentors, and the strength of your Spirit in my life.

Teach me to love like you do.

I ask you to replace my fears with faith, my heartbreak with hope, and my lonely places with your perfect love.

Help me to rise above my fears, and see beyond my limits.

As you refine me through the fire may I remember that your loving discipline will bring about the complete person that you have created for me to be.

Raise my eyes to look beyond the urgent to see what is truly most important. Thank-you, God, that I can face my fears with friendship and faith in YOU. Amen

A Personal Note from Debbie

As we finish the final editing for *Tubular Therapy* I am sitting beside the hospital bed of my daughter, Chelsea. My sweet girl is nineteen years young and she is recovering from complications from a major surgery for Hip Dysplasia. Although Chelsea is nineteen in actual age, she has Down syndrome so she looks at things through the eyes of innocence and with the heart of a sweet child. She trusts in us her parents to protect her. It hurts our hearts that we are not always able to do that as we have watched her suffer greatly.

With a Hoyer lift and the help of many close friends we were able to take care of Chelsea for about a week at home before she became very sick. She was taken by an ambulance to our local hospital. The next day we took her back to Rady's Children's Hospital in San Diego which is one of the best in the country. There she spent a week while they tried to get her little body to function again. From there we were transferred by ambulance to a children's hospital in Orange County which is about 3 ½ hours from home.

Our first night in our new hospital home was one of the longest nights in my entire life. My husband had to leave to go back home to work and we were left to figure out this new world far from home. Our adjoining room was next to a little baby that cries all the time, day and night. We also heard the screams of an older boy who was obviously in a lot of pain. Chelsea was afraid and wanted to go home. I put on her music and headphones to drown out the cries around her. I laid there in the darkness trying to sleep, but I could not. I cried. I prayed. I asked God "why"? Why had things gone wrong? Why were we here? How could we stay here for a month or more?

Alone ... Afraid ... Anxious ... Asking ...

The very next morning I began to meet many of the people that worked at our new hospital home. I had not slept much in the preceding three weeks and all I could do was cry. The workers there were all so very kind. Chelsea's healing has not been quick or instantaneous. Her body HAS begun functioning again, and with the help of physical therapists she is working on trying to scoot out of bed with help and stand for a few minutes on one leg so that she can begin using a walker. She won't be able to begin using her other leg for a while longer. Her journey to healing will be a long painful one.

Let me share with you what I have personally experienced about *Tubular Therapy*.

First, God is here in the midst of pain. He never sleeps or slumbers and His mercies are new every morning. His love is tubular; there is no beginning or end and it surrounds you to keep you afloat.

Second, although God often does not instantaneously stop our pain He does walk through our pain with us.

Third, He is at work even before we can understand what He is doing and why.

Fourth, God uses HIS people to surround us like a big ol' inner tube and keeps us from going under when the waves are surrounding us. He gives us a hand to hold, provides for our real needs, and shows us His amazing love through faithful friends and people that we have just met.

Lastly, God uses suffering to transform us into His likeness. His brand of therapy is not a band aid; He transforms our soul bringing hope, healing, and health to our bodies, our soul, and our emotions. Our brokenness can become a blessing to others. Our mess becomes His finest message! God somehow uses this process and desires us to praise Him and give Him the glory even in the *midst* of the storm.

I want to share with you what God has done in my life just for the asking.

God sent us to a long-term children's hospital that is close to my extended family (my mom, sister and her family, and brother and his wife).

We are also close to the church where we ministered when our kids were young. We have life-long friends here. There has not been a day yet that we have not had visitors bearing gifts, food, goodies, hugs, smiles, and encouragement.

God sent us to a hospital (called Health Bridge) that would allow me to live in Chelsea's room with her and be involved in every moment of her daily care. The very name of the hospital has reminded me of God's plan for each of us. He has provided a bridge for us to walk over that leads us to health and hope.

I could not imagine how different our lives would be right now if we were in a strange town far from home without the people of God to love us, visit us, and minister to our needs. Their love has kept us afloat in extremely turbulent times and has helped us heal.

I have learned a lot in my first week here. Late one night I walked into the bathroom which we share with the crying baby's room. As I listened I heard Christian music playing in her room also. The song that was playing went like this, "Word of God speak. Would you fall down like rain washing my eyes to see Your majesty. Be still and know that You're in this place. Please let me stay and rest in Your holiness. Word of God speak". (As sung by Mercy Me)

I guess I got my answer. Even in the midst of cries, God is here. I found myself praying for the crying baby and her mamma too.

When we first started this endeavor some said, "Why don't you change your title"? They had never heard of *Tubular Therapy (Because we made it up??)* and what did it mean anyway? Retail therapy, now we have all heard of that concept, right? But is there truly healing in faith and friendship?

But the visual of the inner tube holding me up never went away. What kind of therapy was there in Bible times, anyhow? Jesus simply talked with His disciples. He was physically in the boat with them. They never escaped the rough waters, persecution, or even suffering. Yet, they were healed as they faced their fears with faith and boldly praised their God. The world was turned upside down, the church was born, and the good news spread through-out the world.

Tubular Therapy is the story of faith over fear. It is not just a title of a book; it has been the lifeline that has become my testimony. It involves a God who has no limits, His Holy Spirit that lives within me, and friends and family that have walked beside me. I am thankful for best friends, new friends, life-long friends, and my family and church family.

There is a story found in the Old Testament about a man who had leprosy. This man wanted to be healed. The prophet instructed him to go and dip in the dirty Jordon River **seven times**. Why seven times? Would six have done the trick? Not only that, but why didn't the God of the universe just heal this man with his words? Why was action and exact obedience necessary on the part of the leper?

I believe that *Tubular Therapy* is God's way of healing us. Many would prefer to sit in a chair and receive great insight and healing as they understand why things happened as they did. Yet, sadly, I must tell you that most of the people in the Bible did not receive the answer to their "whys". I didn't either; although I certainly asked. If I knew all the pain involved in our long journey I would never have chosen for my daughter to have gone through that surgery or the months that followed. Yet, all of that was required for her to heal and to walk again. God's healing for us often involves floating, trusting, and obedience; we must be willing to walk over His bridge to health. All the while He surrounds us with His unconditional love in the midst of our pain.

Many of us pray for instantaneous healings. We don't want to hurt or suffer. However, in those times of waiting on God as the rapids roll over us we discover what is really needed and what "fluff" is. Like my daughter we will heal one step at a time and that step may take all of our will, mind, strength ... and more.

We are taking life one day at a time. We talk. We trust. We cry. We laugh. We read Get Well cards and look at the pictures sent to us. I appreciate a hot shower when I get one, a little cot on the floor, and any meal that arrives. I thank God for keeping us afloat with His unconditional love and daily faithfulness.

How true it is that we must not go through this journey of life alone because we will all fall down and need a hand up.

Thank God for *Tubular Therapy* as we face our fears with friendship and faith!

The Barefoot Authors

The barefoot authors, Debbie Sempsrott and Denise Rogers, are excited to present three new books in 2013/2014: "Happy Dance", "Tubular Therapy" and "Our Faith Floats".

Each book cover shows feet without shoes. In Exodus 3:5b, Moses encountered Almighty God and was simply told "Take off your sandals, for the place where you are standing is holy ground" (NIV). These images remind us that the same God still speaks, rescues, and provides today. We call ourselves the barefoot authors because *our shoes are off, and we stand in awe of a God that takes the ordinary and turns it into 'Holy Ground'.*

Debbie Sempsrott is a preacher's kid, pastor's wife, and the mother of two. As a mother she has joined the "sisterhood" of special needs, and of adoptive moms. She serves in the area of worship and women's ministries. She is a graduate of Lincoln Christian College (Lincoln, Illinois) and Pacific Christian College (Fullerton, California) with BA's in music and education. She also holds a Master's Degree in Marriage and Family Counseling from Hope International University (Fullerton, California). Most of all she is best known as "Just Debbie". She is the girl next door that loves to play, laugh, and swim in any nearby pool. She is the Ethel who is writing with her best friend, Lucy. She will break the mold on stereotypes for pastors' wives and put the "awe" in each and every story.

Denise Rogers is a graduate of McMurry College (Abilene, Texas). She is an accountant who co-owns her own bookkeeping business. Numbers roll through her mind from morning to night. However, she is not like any accountant you have ever met. She is as funny as the day is long. She has the red hair, antics, and facial expressions of Lucy; and yes, most everyone loves her! Denise is the wife of a "red-neck", mother of a firefighter, a church treasurer, and the person that is called on to speak when they need things to be funny ... really funny. That is the only way "she rolls". She is the queen of Spanx and the one that we call "Funny Denise". After you read a bit, I think you will agree this girl is pure "CWAZEE". She dares to say out-loud what the rest of us only think.

The Barefoot authors' message is one of honesty, hilarity, and hope. Each book contains grins and giggles, tears and triumphs, and hope and healing for the seasons of a woman's soul. You will laugh ... you will cry ... you will laugh until you cry. Your cares will grow smaller, and your view of God will grow larger. When you lay each book down you will simply stand in awe of a God who meets each one of us privately, personally, and providentially. The God of Moses is still alive, real, and intervening in our daily lives. He cares. He comforts. He comes near.

Together our shoes will come off, and we will stand in awe of a God that takes the ordinary and turns it into *'Holy Ground'*.

Denise (left) and Debbie (right) are available to speak for women's events and retreats. You can contact us at www.ourfaithfloats.com.

Totally Tubular Fun

If you enjoyed "Tubular Therapy" we invite you to check out our other books at WestBow Publishing and at Amazon.com.

"Happy Dance"—Fabulous Through the Seasons (Amazon.com)

This book is Grins & Giggles, Tears & Triumphs, and Hope and Healing for the seasons of a woman's soul. We dare not wait for a sunny perfect day that we feel good enough. All of our tomorrows are based on the decisions we make today. If we are to be "fabulous through the seasons" we must take our Heavenly Father's hand, put our feet on His feet and simply learn to follow His leading. Let's celebrate ... It's time to learn to Happy Dance.

"Happy Dance" has been donated to dialysis and cancer centers, Hospice, prisons, Chemo Angels, as well as to women across the country. If you would like to join us in donating books to any of these outreach locations please contact us at <u>www.ourfaithfloats.com.</u>

"Our Faith Floats"—Hope, Hilarity, and Healing for Moms (WestBow Press)

High Stress ... High Seas ...High Hopes ... Never forget who is in your boat! From infertility, adoption, special needs, to the terrible twos and beyond, this book will make you laugh and make you cry; but most of all it will remind you that the God of the universe is right there in your boat! When you are done laughing and crying you will agree with us that our faith floats!

(We invite you to write a book review for us at Amazon.com.)